I0033584

TRANSFORMING PRODUCTS INTO SERVICES

Time to Cross the Rubicon

Paul Jennings

This work is subject to copyright. All rights are solely and exclusively licensed by the Publisher, whether the whole or part of the material is concerned, specifically the rights of translation, reprinting, reuse of illustrations, recitation, broadcasting, reproduction on microfilms or in any other physical way, and transmission or information storage and retrieval, electronic adaptation, computer software, or by similar or dissimilar methodology now known or hereafter developed.

The use of general descriptive names, registered names, trademarks, service marks, etc. in this publication does not imply, even in the absence of a specific statement, that such names are exempt from the relevant protective laws and regulations and therefore free for general use.

The publisher, the authors, and the editors are safe to assume that the advice and information in this book are believed to be true and accurate at the date of publication. Neither the publisher nor the authors or the editors give a warranty, expressed or implied, with respect to the material contained herein or for any errors or omissions that may have been made. The publisher remains neutral with regard to jurisdictional claims in published maps and institutional affiliations.

The author is not an authorised financial or tax advisor. Readers should take independent advice before acting on information contained herein. Information about Tariffs and Net Zero is provided on a best endeavours basis, given the political and policy uncertainty prevailing at the time of writing.

Book Cover by Paul Jennings
Illustrations by Paul Jennings

1st Edition, 2025

Editing, typesetting and publishing by UK Book Publishing
www.ukbookpublishing.com

Copyright © Paul Jennings, ANSENresearch,
Boundary, Staffordshire UK. ST10 2NU

ISBN: 978-1-918077-42-1

www.ansenresearch.co.uk

"Are we really going to try to out-discount low-cost foreign manufacturers?"

Contents

Acknowledgements

There have been so many influences on my progress and preparation of this book. I would like to especially highlight the following people and organisations:

- The Company Team at JCB Finance Ltd.
- Prof. Tim Baines and the Team at the Advanced Services Group, Aston University, Birmingham, UK.
- Lord Bamford DL, Chairman, JCB Group and the Team at JCB Learning Centre.
- The Chartered Institute of Bankers, now the London Institute of Banking & Finance.
- Edward Peck and the Team at Asset Finance Connect.
- Stephen Haddrill, Director General (Ret'd) and the Team at the Finance & Leasing Association, London.
- Gordon Green (now Dec'd), MD and Derek Blood (now Dec'd), Manager at JCB Credit Ltd.
- Mike Ramsay, Persona Training Ltd.
- The Team at the UK Dale Carnegie Organisation.
- The Team at Leadership Development Ltd.
- The Chartered Management Institute.
- Adrian Bennett, Broadwater Training.
- Julian Rose, Director, Asset Finance Policy, UK.

My wife Kath, our daughter Claire and son Andrew – Thank you for your unswerving love and support.

Prologue

In 49BC the Roman General Julius Caesar did the unthinkable of the day. He led his army across the Rubicon River which formed the border between the Roman province of Gaul and Italy.

This immediately posed a threat to Rome itself and was regarded as an act of war, a deliberate act of insurrection against the Senate and the Republic.

Today the phrase to 'Cross the Rubicon' is used to mark an act or moment where a decision or action is taken that is difficult or impossible to reverse. A point of no return is reached.

Perilous risk of staying 'as we are'

How many times do businesses constrain themselves from making the leap from today's time-served situation to meeting tomorrow's needs? The risks of such a transition seemingly outweigh the progress that could ensue. Less regard is paid to the equal (sometimes more perilous) risk of staying 'as we are'.

Foreword

This book explores the dramatically changing market dynamics facing manufacturers and offers answers to the *why and how* to transition to providing 'Advanced Services' to Customers.

The recognised route to market for most manufacturing firms has been through selling goods followed by parts and some longer-term service and maintenance contracts. This has been the standard model for decades.

The advent of products becoming connected through the 'Internet of Things' (IOT) is changing the game and opening up novel opportunities to gain innovative advantage by offering Customers a vast new range of services that could not be provided or even imagined in the past. Whether you are a business leader, team leader, project manager or external consultant, the entrenched model can be incredibly difficult to change.

The following chapters include milestones and materials for senior and middle management, especially in small or medium size firms, to make a leap into Advanced Services.

The Crux of this Book

Beyond the IOT, there are two other important pivotal points facing manufacturers. The new world order of tariffs (which I believe are here to stay) and Net Zero pressures (going beyond government policy) are becoming discernible drivers for change that will prompt Customers to demand other outcomes, going way beyond the mere productive capacity of equipment provided to them.

The Aims of this Book

This book aims to equip manufacturers with a special edge in an increasingly aggressive and contended marketplace by incorporating new or fine-tuning of existing, but often neglected, parts of their business processes.

This includes the urgent need for manufacturers, together with leasing firms, to respond in step to the drivers that are reshaping the traditional trading landscape.

How to Find Ways to Defend Against Low Cost Goods

Find profitable ways to defend against the consequential increase in supply of low-cost, high quality manufactured goods that are seeking replacement markets away from the United States caused by the 'Great Global Tariff Reset'.

How to Find Ways to Grow Via Net Zero

Find profitable ways to grow by seeking fresh, innovative and rewarding opportunities emerging from the onward march of Net Zero caused by government and, in particular, non-government actors.

Servitization - A Key To Unlock the Door

The shift from just making, selling and supporting products to implementing *Servitization*[1] including the provision of advanced services, outcome based contracts, pay-per-use contracts 'X-as-a-Service (XaaS)' contracts is gaining much more attention and offers an important key to unlocking both of the above aims.

A full definition and description of servitization will be covered in a later chapter, but for now, my view is that a multitude of servitization studies have, up to now, understandably concentrated on the complexities of operational business transformation but less focus has been applied to devising the best practices necessary for firms to reshape their internal culture and sales processes to optimise the internal take-up, drafting and selling of servitized contracts.

Funding Platforms to Provide Winning Sales Capabilities

Special focus within this book is applied to finding and adopting a super-smart way of *'taking the money with you'* in Customer sales negotiations. Then to use that new funding platform to support the decision to meet the changing needs of Customers as they move away from mere performance of equipment.

Joining design, manufacturing, sales, marketing, funding and aftermarket service into a more sophisticated and cohesive offering can go on to provide Customers with well-conceived, collaborative, cost justified and guaranteed outcomes – not simply reliable products.

The race is on to capitalise on these changes

The race is on to capitalise on these changes. The winners will create extra beneficial services for their Customers and increased returns for both parties. The losers will likely be left to fight a losing battle against incredibly low-priced commodity goods.

Some issues within the following chapters will be covered in depth and some with a light touch. The light touch issues may well be huge, salient, even global topics in themselves, but are included to add context to the main thrust of the content.

My intention is to include regular personal reflections and demonstrate various issues and solutions through the eyes of employees working for a fictional firm called JENZZO Group. This approach is intended to offer easily digested explanations plus appropriate hints and tips for business owners and their talented teams to DEFEND and GROW in a fundamentally changed market.

It is proper to confirm to the reader that I have an interest here in the work carried out by my consultancy, ANSENresearch, together with the recognised leading authorities on the topic of Servitization at the Advanced Services Group based at Aston University in Birmingham, UK.

Summary & Resources

At the end of each chapter is a brief Summary & Resources section to bring together the ideas covered and other suggested further reading or reference points.

You will note that I use a capital 'C' when referring to a 'Customer' every time. I can't help it – it is so important to treat the term with the reverence it deserves.

A few words are purposely avoided throughout. These are: 'COMPETITOR', 'COMPETITION' and 'COST' (in relation to Customer conversations). Explanations will be provided later but in the meanwhile please put these three words in the sin bin.

This book is not intended to be a scholarly or authoritative standalone account of Servitization.

[1] More information is available at:
https://www.advancedservicesgroup.co.uk/

CHAPTER 1

Thriving Inside a New World Order

Despite the financial crash of 2008 and its aftershocks, we may look back on the first part of the twenty-first century as a golden era of low inflation caused by Governments and Central Banks around the world running low interest rates coupled with an abundant supply of low-cost and increased quality of Chinese manufactured goods being delivered via massively enmeshed and complex supply chains.

But the whole system came to a sudden halt in 2020 with the arrival of the Coronavirus pandemic. Shortage of supplies of many raw materials and finished goods (compounded by war in Ukraine) caused further stress and led to the resurgence of inflation.

A thought occurred to me at the time that China would learn from this experience and use the West's dependence on their near-monopoly of some manufactured goods as a future potential geopolitical weapon to purposely create inflation in those economies almost at will. By imposing export taxes on their own manufacturers, knowing that alternative suppliers would not be able to replace the supply of these goods at short notice or similar prices, China could cause disruption and social unrest in selected economies on demand.

What I didn't see, with any clarity, was the possibility that the largest importing economy, the United States, would do the reverse and self-impose swingeing import taxes (tariffs) on Chinese manufactured goods, alongside sweeping tariffs across global trade.

As trading with the US economy becomes more challenging in the short and medium term, maybe even closed to some goods manufactured in lower-cost economies, where will be the alternative target markets for these goods and what will be the consequences for domestic manufacturers as more low-cost and high quality goods get redirected away from the US market? [1]

According to figures from Chinese customs, exports from China to the EU increased by 8.2% in April 2025 compared with April 2024. At the member state level, exports to Germany rose by 20.4% over the same period, while the Netherlands saw an increase of 5.6%, Italy 4.7%, and France 2.6%. In the meantime, Chinese exports to the US have fallen by 20% over the same period.[2] In response, the EU have set up a monitoring centre to assess the threat.

"Are we really going to try to out-discount low-cost foreign manufacturers?"

Prior to the added pressure of the emerging new world trade position, I frequently used a question to illustrate the need for a pivot point for domestic manufacturers – "Are we really going to try to out-discount low-cost foreign manufacturers?"

This is obviously a fruitless route to follow and will end in failure. The need for change is urgent and necessary. A strong counter, that is difficult to replicate, is an expansion of services running alongside products or even becoming the main proposition for dealing with Customers in the future. Reconfiguring a business to compete on advanced services is a challenge and, once embraced, there is no way back, hence the 'Rubicon needs to be crossed'.

what is the plan to grapple with these changed dynamics?

Therefore, what is the plan to grapple with these changed dynamics? The first challenge of strategic change can sometimes seem daunting because changing processes and even a way of life is not a simple or easy matter. Many business owners are strong characters – they may have created unswerving certainty and tradition about what they feel should be done and require that other people within their business fall in line. Challenging that central certainty is difficult.

The second part is about changing the mindsets of groups of key people – the *'stakeholders'* – which can be another challenge in itself. The question arises about "how can I create a successful and lasting change within my business?". This becomes even more of an issue if you have been placed in charge of a transformation project within a larger established business with many other co-workers holding views about what to do.

Further considerations might be:
- Is our project meant to defend our business or help it grow, or both?
- The project might feel overwhelming.
- How do I manage stakeholders?
- What authority do I have? Who can I turn to?
- What are our firm's real skills and capabilities?
- Are there any capabilities we've not identified or chosen not to exploit so far – and why?
- Where could we open up a route to more revenue?
- Can we expand our Customer offer beyond selling goods together with parts and some warranty aftercare?
- Is the transition to Net Zero seen as a threat or an opportunity for our business and our Customers?
- How does our bank treat us?

The list can go on...

Life of a Special Project

There's a long running old quip about the 'Life of a Special Project' that goes something like this:
- **Initial Enthusiasm** quickly changing to...
- **Disillusionment**, turning into...
- **Panic**, followed by a...

- **Search for the Guilty**
- **Punishment of the Innocent** and ultimately...
- **Promotion of the Non-Participants**

There are various versions but as we shall see, there are some processes and behaviours that can avoid some of this brutality!

I've enjoyed meeting and doing business with hundreds of business leaders over the years. It has paid to listen to them. The most successful business leaders I've met are extremely driven individuals – they have no 'off-button' especially if they're running a family business. They are completely dedicated to building something from nothing or strengthening a company or family business handed down to them and have a heritage to protect.

The most successful business leaders
I've met are extremely driven
individuals – they have no 'off-button'

They are continuously absorbing government intervention, policy changes, tightening regulation, tax expansion, health & safety requirements, recruitment of qualified staff, diversity & inclusion issues, raw materials inflation and energy costs to name but a few. Shareholder demands and the speed of changes in technology plus increasing market tensions add to the spinning plates.

We will be delving into the considerations raised in this short chapter plus more as we progress through matters that, perhaps at first, appear to be separate and unrelated. My intention is to bring them together as we look at transforming into modern performance and find a path to thrive inside the new world order.

Summary & Resources

The new world order for trade, ushered in by the USA will not be a flash in the pan – the tectonic plates have shifted. Commercial allies and foes have both been bruised, and trading tensions will remain. New alliances, such as BRICS[3] and ASEAN[4], are gaining either membership and/or momentum, and other countries will have to look further afield for markets for their goods.

Developed countries who remain within the sphere of some form of free trade are bound to feel more heat from low-cost producers as goods deflect from the world's largest importing nation – the USA.

Thriving within this new world order will require changes beyond simple pricing tactics to give manufacturers space to both defend and grow market share and revenue.

[1] *US trade war could divert Chinese goods to EU markets.*
https://hongkongfp.com/2025/04/12/
us-trade-war-could-divert-chinese-goods-to-eu-markets-analysts-say/

[2] *Increase in Chinese export threat to EU:*
https://www.euronews.com/my-europe/2025/06/05/tariffs-commis-
sion-strengthens-imports-monitoring-amid-fear-of-trade-diversion

[3] *BRICS Expansion & Future etc:*
https://carnegieendowment.org/research/2025/03/
brics-expansion-and-the-future-of-world-order-perspectives-
from-member-states-partners-and-aspirants?lang=en

[4] *World Economic Forum ASEAN Article:*
https://www.weforum.org/stories/2025/07/
why-asean-must-transform-global-tensions-into-regional-opportunities/

CHAPTER 2

The Net Zero Challenge

The idea of reducing the amount of Green House Gases (GHG) to slow down global warming is a simple idea — less CO_2 emissions equals less warming. The problem is the radical action that is required to get the correct level of reduction. It is a daunting prospect and is occupying governments, lobbyists, other authorities and sceptics around the world.

It is not the intention of this chapter to delve into the controversies surrounding the topic but to give a sense of the sheer magnitude and momentum of the march to Net Zero. We will need to look at some of these driving forces, many of which are now completely outside the control of governments, and we will go on to explore some ways that Servitization can be coupled with the Net Zero ambition to create areas of innovative growth opportunities.

The context of this chapter will benefit from some detailed definitions and related Net Zero pressure points so that we can better understand what is already in train. There's a lot to take in, some of it is heavy going – so stick with it, and here goes.

Conference of the Parties (COP)

The supreme decision-making body of the United Nations Framework Convention on Climate Change (UNFCCC) is the COP[1]. All States that are parties to the Convention are represented at the COP, at which they review the implementation of the Convention and any other legal instruments that the COP adopts, and take decisions necessary to promote the effective implementation of the Convention, including institutional and administrative arrangements. The regular Conventions bring together countries to negotiate and implement agreements aimed at addressing climate change, eg limiting global warming to no more than 1.5°C.

Science Based Targets Initiative (SBTi)

SBTi[2] is a corporate climate action organisation that enables companies and financial institutions worldwide to play their part in combating the climate crisis. It develops standards, tools and guidance which allow companies to set Green House Gas (GHG) emissions reductions targets in line with what is needed to keep global heating below catastrophic levels and reach net-zero by 2050 at the latest.

This initiative provides for companies to state their ambition to reduce GHG emissions between a base year

and a target year. The SBTi organisation maintains that adopting targets:
- Boosts profitability.
- Improves investor confidence.
- Drives innovation.
- Reduces regulatory uncertainty.
- Strengthens brand reputation.

Setting aside the 'SBTi' wrapper, the above outcomes are also key focus areas of this book.

An example of a commitment currently recorded in the SBTi database is as follows:

"LG Electronics Inc. commits to reduce absolute scope 1 and scope 2 GHG emissions 54.6% by 2030 from a 2017 base year. LG Electronics Inc. also commits to reduce scope 3 GHG emissions from use of sold products 20% per functional unit sold by 2030 from a 2020 base year."

GHG Emission Scopes

GHG emissions are defined by the Green House Gas Protocol and categorised into three 'Scopes' as shown in the graphic (See Figure 1).
- **Scope 1** - Direct emissions from owned or controlled sources.
- **Scope 2** - Indirect emissions from purchased energy.
- **Scope 3** - All other indirect emissions in the value chain.

At the time of writing there are 306 organisations classified as banks, diverse financials and insurance on the SBTi database. Examples include the UK-based NatWest Bank, Dutch-based ING, Swiss Re, and Hong Kong-based AIA Group. The database discloses whether GHG reduction targets, to meet Net Zero by 2050, have been set, committed or commitment removed.

GHG Emissions Across the Value Chain

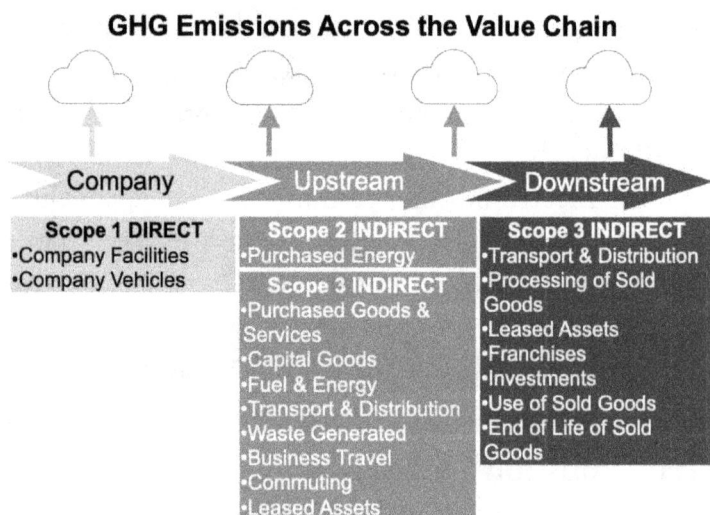

Company	Upstream	Downstream
Scope 1 DIRECT •Company Facilities •Company Vehicles	**Scope 2 INDIRECT** •Purchased Energy **Scope 3 INDIRECT** •Purchased Goods & Services •Capital Goods •Fuel & Energy •Transport & Distribution •Waste Generated •Business Travel •Commuting •Leased Assets	**Scope 3 INDIRECT** •Transport & Distribution •Processing of Sold Goods •Leased Assets •Franchises •Investments •Use of Sold Goods •End of Life of Sold Goods

Figure 1: Simplified GHG Scopes

Organisations that fail to submit targets within 24 months of making a commitment are identified with a 'Commitment Removed' record in the dashboard. Several financial organisations including Aegon Nederland N.V., Germany's Allianz Investment Management SE, Spain's BBVA, UK's Standard Chartered Bank are now recorded in this way.

SBTi Targets

Targets are clearly-defined, science-based pathways for companies and financial institutions to decarbonise their operations and value chains, which have been reviewed and validated by SBTi Services.

The amount of work to undertake these requirements, for example, within a major bank or insurance company is huge. The basic needs are to calculate the various GHG Scope emissions from their operations and their whole Customer portfolio from a start-point (the Base Year), say 2019 and then make near-term (say 2030) and long-term commitments to reduce these emissions to net zero by 2050.

A simplistic example for a bank or insurance company means trying to assess the level of GHG emissions related to their involvement with all Customers in 2019 and then to manage a reduction of those emissions to 50% of that total by 2030. The question arises around the word 'manage'. Does this mean encouraging Customers to swap to green energy sources for their operations and products, or does it mean abandoning Customers who have no plans or lack sufficient progress to move their GHG emissions quickly enough?

Perhaps the banks and insurers who have had SBTi target commitments removed may have found that the calculation and monitoring exercise would be an impossible burden for them or the consequences of 'managing' their portfolios, ie Customer affairs, would be commercially damaging for both parties. Time will tell.

Task Force on Climate-related Financial Disclosures - TCFD

The Financial Stability Board (FSB) created the TCFD[3] to develop recommendations on the types of information that companies should disclose to support investors, lenders, and insurance underwriters in appropriately assessing and pricing a specific set of risks related to climate change. The FSB arranged for the IFRS Foundation to take over the monitoring of the progress of companies' climate-related disclosures.

The International Financial Reporting Standards Foundation (IFRS)[4] is a not-for-profit, public interest organisation established to develop high-quality, under-standable, enforceable and globally accepted accounting and sustainability disclosure standards.

Their Standards are developed by two standard-setting boards, the International Accounting Standards Board (IASB) and International Sustainability Standards Board (ISSB).

IFRS standards are mandatory in many parts of the world, especially for large or publicly quoted companies. Smaller businesses can follow localised standards. The US uses a different standards system called Generally Accepted Accounting Principles (GAAP). Adopting accounting standards allows any external party to assess the standing of a business in a consistent way.

Those businesses around the world that are required to publish their annual accounts in accordance with IFRS standards have had two important new sustainability/

climate related disclosures to follow from 2024 – IFRS S1 and S2.

IFRS S1[5]. General Requirements for Disclosure of Sustainability-related Financial Information provides a set of disclosure requirements designed to enable companies to communicate to investors about the sustainability-related risks and opportunities they face over the short, medium and long term.

IFRS S2[6]. Climate-related Disclosures sets out specific climate-related disclosures and is designed to be used with IFRS S1.

UK Sustainability Reporting Standards

In November 2024, a press notice accompanying the Chancellor's Mansion House speech spoke about "our ambition to deliver a world-leading sustainable finance framework", including consulting "on economically significant companies disclosing information using future UK Sustainability Reporting Standards"[7]. The UK government will publish finalised versions of UK SRS S1 and UK SRS S2 for voluntary use later this year. Subsequently, the government and the Financial Conduct Authority (FCA) will consider whether to introduce requirements for certain UK entities to report against these standards.

Streamlined Energy & Carbon Reporting (SECR)

From financial years beginning on or after 1 April 2019,

SECR[8] required large UK companies to report publicly on their UK energy use and carbon emissions within their Directors' Report.

SECR impacts any companies, LLPs and groups that exceed at least two of the following three thresholds in the financial year:
- £36m annual turnover
- £18m balance sheet total
- 250 employees

For businesses meeting the above criteria, company or group reporting is required regardless of whether an overseas parent company or group has published a similar report. A group may, however, exclude any energy and carbon information relating to any subsidiaries which would not be obliged to report individually according to the thresholds. After undertaking a calculation, where a company has consumed less than 40MWh, a disclosure is not required.

The inclusion of energy use and carbon emissions in UK company accounts will lay bare the firm's position in relation to Net Zero commitments enabling all of its stakeholders to form an opinion as to whether or not to support its on-going operations. Forming an opinion on a single first statement covering one year will not be the pivotal moment, but a trend will be visible as years mount up. This will prove awkward for firms that are growing either organically or by acquisition because GHG emissions could be seen to rise rather than fall even if conscientious action is being taken, whereas a company that is shrinking will naturally be reporting lower emissions even if no commitment is taking place on reduction of GHG.

A good example of greenhouse gas and energy consumption reporting can be found in the Statutory Annual accounts filed for Cemex Operations UK Ltd to 31st December 2023[9]. This company is a subsidiary of a global cement and concrete products manufacturer. A wide array of information is provided to show performance within each Scope including consumption of electricity and natural gas plus emissions from other activities, and this enables shareholders, financiers, insurers, employees, suppliers and Customers to quickly see whether progress in GHG reductions are being made, which in this case appear to be moving in the desired direction.

Evidence of a lack of knowledge held by UK SMEs about Net Zero issues is contained in a survey published in August 2025 by the UK's Aldermore Bank – *Green SME Index*[10] which showed the following:

- Only 13% of SMEs are truly net zero ready as the number of businesses 'going green' stagnates, raising concerns ahead of incoming UK Sustainability Reporting Standards (UKSRS).
- A quarter of SMEs (24%) are assessing 'green goals' but 76% are yet to act
- Two-thirds of SMEs have never heard of Scope 1, 2 or 3 emissions, despite upcoming requirements
- SMEs see sustainability as a barrier (82%) to their business but believe 'going green' could add £52k to bottom lines annually.

Stakeholder Activism

Banks & Insurance Companies - This was also mentioned briefly under the SBTi heading. Banks calculate Green House Gas (GHG) emissions from their portfolios, primarily focusing on "financed emissions", which are the emissions associated with the companies they finance or invest in. This calculation involves identifying the banks' exposure to specific companies or sectors and then applying emission factors to estimate the emissions linked to that exposure. Techniques like the Partnership for Carbon Accounting Financials (PCAF)[11] methodology are used to standardise this process.

For a moment, let's suppose we sit on the Board of a bank. We may have large blocks of shareholders who are pension fund investors who are quite vocal Net Zero activists. Our policy is to meet Net Zero emissions from our portfolio of Customers by 2050 (an overall target set into UK law). We may choose a baseline of say 2019 against which to measure progress of Scopes 1-3 by setting an interim target of a 50% reduction in GHG by 2030 and measure our performance along the way using PCAF methods. This means that we are going to have to try to calculate what our financed portion of each Customer's emissions were in 2019 and then track this in the future to determine whether or not we wish to continue to support this Customer and/or the type of assets related to our financial support. Our bank also uses Credit Reference Agencies such as Equifax who are also gathering such information as part of broadening their services[12].

If our interim target is to be met, when do we begin to introduce weighting factors in our decision-making on medium-term or long-term loans and investments proposed by our Customers? In other words, if we receive an application to fund a €100m fleet of diesel trucks today for a Customer on seven-year terms, the GHG emissions will have a detrimental impact on the bank's ability to meet our own 2030 50% GHG reduction target. The trucks will continue to emit the same GHG levels within our portfolio beyond 2030 and so will we lend now or not? It is a tricky question. For the time being, perhaps it may cause a 'little blurring' of progress on our bank's targeting commitments? Could we expect some 'anti-trust' actions against us for being accused of unfairly treating an otherwise viable Customer by refusing to lend them the money? Other groups within our shareholders may question our actions too. The same questions about providing cover will be troubling insurance Board rooms.

Shareholders - Pension funds, institutional investors, private investors and directors. These actors are obviously very powerful influencers, either directly by applying pressure on company Boards or via their enthusiasm or otherwise to buy shares affecting the market share price.

Employees - The days of committing to a long career with a single employer are mostly over. Key employees with highly portable skills and radical or even moderate personal views about climate change will be able to see their employer's Net Zero progress even if 'green-washed' internal communications are circulated. Attracting the right talent could become more challenging. This type of pressure has been seen with the pivot to home-working for millions of employees. Interviewees expect genuine flexibility and voice their demands at the recruitment stage. Employer commitments to Net Zero have also entered onto their list of questions at interview.

Customers - Customers may be experiencing the same Net Zero pressures as the supplier. This could prompt questions and demands about GHG reductions in suppliers' energy sources (Scope 1), operations (scope 2) and their products (Scope 3). Imagine an architect being instructed by their client that a new stadium or university research centre must be built with Net Zero credentials? It is unsurprising that companies such as Cemex wish to publish the positive actions they are taking to aid this scenario.

Suppliers - See comments relating to Customers.

Media - It would be remiss of companies to ignore the influence of the media, be it traditional national press, specialist industry sector publications or social media. Businesses could be exposed to concerted reputational damage if decisions or progress on climate change are not taken seriously, especially if the number of extreme weather events or other natural difficulties continue to be pinned down to climate change.

Environmental, Social and Governance (ESG)

ESG[13] is a set of standards measuring a business's impact on society, the environment, and how transparent and accountable it is. Despite its good intentions, ESG has been receiving some bad press recently, particularly in the

USA[14] where it is perceived as part of a liberal and divisive agenda. More than 30 states have introduced anti-ESG legislation. Some large organisations have withdrawn from recognising the main principles.

Making ESG data available in public facing company briefings is intended to confirm commitment to acting and trading in an ethical way. These data can be used by stakeholders who are interested in trading, investing or becoming employees. Scores can be attached to the data which then makes it theoretically even easier to pass judgement.

- **Environmental** - Scores look at how the firm approaches guardianship of the environment.
- **Social** - Scores evidence the firm's relationships with employees, suppliers, Customers, and communities.
- **Governance** - Records the firm's leadership, executive pay, audits and internal controls and shareholder rights.

Investment companies, pension funds, brokers and other stakeholders can therefore decide whether or not to trade with firms based on their own set of ESG beliefs and standards.

Aside from environmental issues covered above, an example would be a Pension Fund deciding that it didn't want to invest their members' funds into arms manufacturers. This can lead to quandaries, for instance, is it ethical to invest in armaments where the weapons are needed to protect the democratic rights of another state or indeed, the existence of the home country? In the UK during World War II, it was a patriotic duty to invest in 'War Bonds'.

Sustainable Development Goals

The 2030 Agenda for Sustainable Development[15] adopted by all United Nations Member States in 2015, provides a shared blueprint for peace and prosperity for people and the planet, now and into the future. At its heart are the 17 Sustainable Development Goals (SDGs), which are an urgent call for action by all countries – developed and developing – in a global partnership. See Figure 2: https://www.un.org/sustainabledevelopment

Figure 2: The 17 SDG Goals

They recognise that ending poverty and other deprivations must go hand-in-hand with strategies that improve health and education, reduce inequality, and spur economic growth – all while tackling climate change and working to preserve our oceans and forests.

A Report prepared jointly between the European Banking Federation (EBF) and KPMG[16] in June 2021 surveyed 48 banks. When asked *"has your bank publicly pledged to meet certain sustainability targets in its lending portfolio?"*, almost half responded *"Yes, and those targets trickle down through all our business units (retail, wealth and asset management, consumer finance, corporate and investment banking, etc".*

The survey went on to ask, *"Which SDGs have the greatest relevance for the sector?"*. The top two SDG considerations were: 83% Decent Work and Economic Growth and 75% Climate Action. Various other questions confirmed a high degree of commitment including Board involvement in adopting and monitoring SDG performance across banks in Europe.

Net Zero Paradox

In the meantime, we are seeing either push-back or even rejoicing at *"Drill Baby, Drill"* and new coal production records are being hit and lauded in some countries.

> *"Drill Baby, Drill" and new coal production records are being hit in other countries*

In 2023, China was by far the largest consumer of coal in the world. That year, the country used some 4.99 billion metric tons of the fossil fuel, which translated to more than half of total worldwide coal consumption. India and the United States followed as the second and third largest coal consumers.[17]

The question of achieving global Net Zero in developed countries through unilateral action can be seen as a somewhat forlorn task given that China, India and other developing countries with high populations have an understandable desire to improve the welfare of their citizens through a dash for provision of electrical power. This obviously undermines the overall environmental concerns being addressed by COP unless the dash for power is seen to be provided by green sources in the near future.

However, as can be seen in the range of initiatives described above, the Net Zero course has been set for many countries around the world and GHG reductions will remain a driver for change, either through or irrespective of policies set by governments.

By way of example, major manufacturers of cars and trucks are demonstrating how implementing strategic change (through battery or other drivetrain fuels) takes enormous investment and long lead times. Governments may jiggle different Net Zero targets in attempts to accommodate some of this, but there are many other influences that will propel change and make the process increasingly inevitable.

In which case, what kind of design, manufacture and trading tactics can be employed to handle this dynamic? How does a business transform itself to compete when strict protocols apply from SBTi, Scopes 1, 2 & 3, IFRS, SECR, ESG, SDG and many other regimes from banking and insurance appetite, to shareholder, employee and consumer pressures?

How can businesses equip themselves against this quandary especially when weighed against imported goods which may well have been produced using much lower cost (but CO_2 emitting) energy and lower labour costs?

Net Zero & Servitization Opportunities

The Net Zero drivers covered above, are not exhaustive but demonstrate that companies, whether manufacturers or end users, are facing, or will face, unparalleled pressures that have no equal in historic trading conditions. At times such as these, the more agile and responsive firms will be recognising new business opportunities. These are likely to take the form of helping end users to meet their own GHG obligations as government and non-government initiatives take hold in the short and medium term.

Manufacturers will be caught in the cross-hairs of reducing their own GHG emissions footprint but also their activities which include responsibility for reporting on emissions resulting from the goods that they have sold plus responsibilities for dealing with end of life of those goods.

Increasingly important outcomes will be based on Net Zero credentials

Net Zero Outcomes

Designing goods for outcomes will stretch focus beyond improving the performance and serviceability of goods, it will include parameters that aid both the manufacturer and end user to make continuous improvements toward

Net Zero targets until the end of working life for products.

Increasingly important outcomes will be based on Net Zero credentials to enable reporting such things as:

- Fuel efficiency/GHG reductions.
- Fuel agnostic or multi fuel equipment.
- More electrification and Hydrogen power.
- In-life continuous improvement.
- More operational automation and AI integration.
- Increased circularity to allow for more efficient and extended utilisation.
- Increased durability and refurbishment of products.
- Waste reduction.
- Provision of more operational efficiency data.
- Capture of Scope 1, 2, 3 data.

These outcomes open up a new realm of advance services and manufacturers would be wise to research how these characteristics can be built into current R&D thinking.

The issues involved are not typical engineering considerations and much thought will need to be given to the array of Net Zero pressure points to arrive at a new set of design questions requiring useful solutions. Many Customers may not yet have seen what is coming down the track in the form of their stakeholders making new and unprecedented demands, and so product research will have to bear this in mind.

New capabilities will be required within manufacturing firms to allow them to absorb and translate oncoming demands and needs emanating from Net Zero pressures.

Summary & Resources

Eventually, very few businesses will be immune from Net Zero demands through various actors involved in a powerful pincer movement.

This chapter has attempted to provide a broad background to some of the main Net Zero drivers and the growing range of pressure points causing firms to urgently review their position on GHG emissions and use of other natural resources.

The need to assess what and how products are made to emit less GHG during their working lifetimes and to extend product lifetimes to bring about 'Circularity' is becoming an urgent topic. Providing deeper service levels combined with closer consultation with Customers (and suppliers) could lead to providing a new realm of advanced services that include outcomes related to the Net Zero goals of Customers. This is a platform that could further add to positional advantage and improved returns. It ties in directly with Servitization which lies at the heart of this book.

Net Zero web resources already mentioned in this chapter are shown in the following table. The list is not intended to be exhaustive or a definitive account but merely offers a summary to what is a huge and growing topic.

N	Regime	Net Zero Web Resource Table
1	COP	https://unfccc.int/process/bodies/ supreme-bodies/conference-of-the-parties-cop
2	SBTi	https://sciencebasedtargets.org/
3	TCFD	https://www.fsb-tcfd.org/
4	IFRS/ISSB	https://www.ifrs.org/sustainability/tcfd/
5	IFRS S1	https://www.ifrs.org/issued-standards/ ifrs-sustainability-standards-navigator/ ifrs-s1-general-requirements/
6	IFRS S2	https://www.ifrs.org/issued-standards/ ifrs-sustainability-standards-navigator/ ifrs-s2-climate-related-disclosures/
7	UKSRS	https://www.gov.uk/guidance/ uk-sustainability-reporting-standards
8	SECR/ PwC	https://www.pwc.co.uk/services/audit/ non-financial-assurance/streamlined-en- ergy-and-carbon-reporting.html
9	Cemex	https://find-and-update.company-information. service.gov.uk/company/00658390/filing-history
10	Aldermore Green SME Index	https://www.aldermore.co.uk/ newsroom/smes-face-net-zero-divide- as-2026-green-reporting-looms/
11	PCAF	https://carbonaccountingfinancials.com/
12	Equifax	https://www.equifax.co.uk/business/ blog/-/insight/article/measuring-the-invisi- ble-how-banks-calculate-financed-emissions/
13	ESG	https://www.british-business-bank.co.uk/ business-guidance/guidance-articles/sustainability/ what-is-esg-a-guide-for-smaller-businesses
14	ESG in USA	https://www.azeusconvene.com/en-gb/ articles/the-state-of-esg-in-the-u-s- and-how-its-impacting-europe
15	SDG	https://sdgs.un.org/goals
16	EFB/ KPMG	https://www.ebf.eu/wp-content/ uploads/2021/06/European-bank-practices- in-supporting-and-implementing-the-UN- Sustainable-Development-Goals.pdf
17	Coal	Garside www.statista.com

CHAPTER 3

Fourth Industrial Revolution

If you're new to this, it sounds very grand! The name is meant to define the current evolutionary state of manufacturing of which I'm not an expert, but the general topic has relevance and context to the rest of the book.

The First Industrial Revolution in the early to mid 1800s involved the transition from handmade products to water and steam powered mass-production. The arrival of these new technologies is attributed to a stream of inventions developed in the United Kingdom.

The Second, sometimes called the 'Technological Revolution' during the late 1800s onwards, involved the introduction of transport improvements such as railways, steam powered maritime transport, telegraph networks, electrification and the development of production line techniques.

The Third is characterised by the term 'Digital Revolution' which began in the late 20th century and involved the growth of information technology, the internet and digitalised communications combined with industrial processes.

The Fourth is considered separate to the third by virtue of the speed of the adoption and power of modern 'cyber-physical systems' (CPS). It is often abbreviated to 'Industry 4.0' or '4IR' or other nomenclature[1].

Some of the main components are widely recognised by the general public via mobile telephony and smart-phones allowing hyper connectivity to a multitude of places, people and things.

The web and other resources are full of descriptions about what 4IR covers, but for the purpose of this book we need to recognise the early strategic actions and implementation of it by the German government in 2011. It is significant that Germany is a high-cost centre of quality engineering and the pursuit of 4IR techniques was no doubt seen as a way to help create and preserve manufacturer advantage in the production of finished goods. However, even though high capital cost is involved, the components and approach are not unique. How quickly have or will developing economies adopt it and succeed?

Smart Factories, Robots, 3D Printing, Artificial Intelligence, Smart Sensors and Predictive Maintenance are all common features of 4IR. It is the final three that find room in the underlying message of this book.

Manufacturing processes have become copied or moved around the world. The early British inventors and adopters of the First Industrial Revolution were textile manufacturers. The production of cloth by sophisticated water powered and then steam powered machinery saw incredible increases in the availability and affordability of quality cloth. Their dominance in this industry, based on supplies of raw cotton mostly from the USA, was undisputed for a long time and accounted for 42%[2] of Britain's exports.

That dominance was eventually undermined by diffusion of know-how

Despite the British imposing government controls on exports of machinery and artisans, that dominance was eventually undermined by diffusion of know-how which led, in simplistic terms, to textiles being manufactured using the improved production techniques closer to the source of raw materials, for instance in India.

The German 4IR initiative aimed to create an edge for its economic bias in engineering and exporting brilliance and offer protection for domestic manufacturers, although this has been widely studied and the techniques and benefits emulated around the world. This prompts the question 'where to next?'.

Industry 5.0?

In 2021, the European Commission formally called for the Fifth Industrial Revolution (Industry 5.0). A document entitled 'Industry 5.0: Towards a Sustainable, Human-centric, and Resilient European Industry'[3] was published in January 2021. The main aims, as the title suggests, are sustainability, human-centricity and resilience, harnessing the power of industry to achieve societal goals beyond jobs and growth, to become a resilient provider of prosperity and encouraging manufacturers to respect the limits of the natural world whilst respecting the welfare of workers at the core of the production process.

Competing Against Comparable Goods

There is a message here for domestic manufacturers in that trading against comparable imported goods purely on finished product features, benefits and price is extremely tough. Developing attractive brand presence is, of course, a well-used defensive strategy, providing enough followers can be convinced to be long-term consumers and ambassadors for the products.

The objective is to provide 'usership' rather than ownership.

There is another important approach to engaging with Customers that aims to deliver mutual benefits for manufacturers and Customers alike which is often over-looked or, because of its business transformational needs, is considered too difficult to implement. This method extends way beyond a prime focus on the product's features and benefits, and embraces or over-arches the life-span of the product by aiming to help the Customer to derive superior outputs from the use of the product. The objective is to provide 'usership' rather than ownership. This ties in well with re-use and refurbishment of equipment after the first usership term expires and plays into the increasingly important theme of 'Circularity'[4].

An often cited example is the way Rolls-Royce provide their aero engines via 'Power by the Hour' contracts to ensure and <u>guarantee</u> the best possible fuel efficiency, availability, reliability and up-time for the airlines who use their products, thereby creating a type of ring-fence around the route to the Customer as long as that service excellence and economic soundness is continuously provided. The contractual outcome has sometimes been impertinently described as 'the Customer is buying hot air'. That is, the jet propulsion provided by the reliable Rolls-Royce engines.

In other words, the manufacturer is taking on a more complex undertaking and set of risks to guarantee valuable operational outcomes from its products. This approach is far more difficult to copy and conversely very easy to get wrong in the Customers' eyes – hence the risk label applied above.

The term given to this type of trading arrangement is SERVITIZATION, which is explored in the next chapter.

Summary & Resources

Many manufacturers and national governments are committed to heavily investing in state-of-the-art production techniques with a view to gaining advantages in the marketplace and perhaps build in ecological and social considerations. The topic is huge and is the subject of enormous study and literature, and this chapter merely scratches the surface.

The question is how quickly innovative production methods can be replicated within global supply chains consequently diminishing the temporary advantage gained. If this is so, how do manufacturers in the future distinguish their products in a way that is hard to copy?

Further reading, see:

[1] *The Fourth Industrial Revolution*
https://www.interaction-design.org/literature/
topics/the-fourth-industrial-revolution?

[2] *The Cotton Industry in Britain*
https://www.historic-uk.com/HistoryUK/
HistoryofBritain/Cotton-Industry/

[3] *Industry 5.0: Towards a Sustainable, Human-centric, and Resilient European Industry*
https://research-and-innovation.ec.europa.eu/news/
all-research-and-innovation-news/industry-50-towards-more-sustainable-resilient-and-human-centric-industry-2021-01-07_en

[4] *Circularity*
https://www.ellenmacarthurfoundation.org/topics/
circular-economy-introduction/overview

CHAPTER 4

The Pivot to Providing Services

S ervitization sets out to accomplish many important things for both manufacturers and Customers. The impact goes far beyond the traditional sales model, which, I've heard, can be cheekily summed up as "Flog some gear, sell some parts and maybe try for a service contract".

"Flog some gear, sell some parts and maybe try for a service contract"

Sad to say that I've even witnessed the idea of selling service contracts as a last-ditch attempt to rescue a failing capital sale! A bit like enticing a horse onto a trailer with a last-minute carrot dangled at its rear end! It is almost sure to fail and eventually it doesn't matter how many other carrots (trading discount) are offered once understanding, direction and credibility are lost in the negotiation. The nature and pivot point of the horse negotiation and outcome was always going to be needed at the front end, carrot first. This analogy has meaning elsewhere in the book.

Definition of Servitization

Servitization[1] is a transformation process through which a manufacturing company changes its business model to compete through a bundle of products and services, rather than products alone.

Advanced Services are outcome-based offerings that help manufacturers' Customers be more successful. These services focus on delivering outcomes from the product usage rather than selling product ownership, creating maximum value for the Customers *and* the manufacturers.

The 'Great 2025 Global Tariff Shock' - Defensive Action

The 'Great Global Tariff Shock' will place pressure on low-cost production countries to re-direct their sales to countries who have less aggressive tariff regimes, which will place even more pressure on domestic manufacturers who may compete mainly on price.

There has to be another way, and providing and deepening services will be the answer in many cases. In my experience, a route to recognising the scope and opportunities of Servitization can initially grow from small ideas within a company environment. It is by no means a certainty that companies grasp and take forward these ideas; however, it may be a fatal mistake to think that a firm should carry on attempting to fight a simple price discounting war with other suppliers.

Introducing the 'JENZZO' Project Team

Here we begin a fictitious example of changing or pivoting a manufacturer's perspective.

A product development team within a family owned, global manufacturer called JENZZO Group have been formed to design, manufacture and market a new product adding to JENZZO's wide portfolio which includes port handling equipment, rail yard logistics equipment, waste recovery and municipal equipment, with worldwide distribution supported by a network of seven regional offices and teams. The new product is an Airport Tug. The kind of machine that tows expensive aircraft around an airport ramp. It is a first attempt by JENZZO to enter this sector.

Mike is the Project Leader, **Todd** is the Chief Development Engineer, **Sam** has been drafted in from the Service & After-Market Division. **Amy** is the Marketing Lead and, unusually for this type of project, **Sylvia** has been drafted in from their current independent asset finance partner, Colaborar Leasing (C Leasing), which is the asset financing subsidiary of Colaborar Bank (C Bank). Sylvia's company are a major provider of leasing facilities to a number of manufacturers in many international markets. They don't usually get to be part of such a development team.

Let us enter their latest regular meeting that has just started.

Mike is happy with engineering progress so far and is pleased that their new airport tug offers some distinct design benefits on speed and weight capacity plus a new suite of telematics – JENZZO have arrived at last at the 'internet of things' (IoT). However, he's concerned that their costings are out of line with the market leader for airport tugs. These units are predominantly sold on 'Contract Hire' by intermediary suppliers (specialist hirers of airport handling equipment) and they often act as a block on the route to market.

Amy's market intelligence work has established that the market leader's specialist products (without telematics) are currently being provided to airport operators via equipment rental firms for around €700 per week fully maintained on seven-year terms. Using the estimated retail prices of our machine and the service costs plus the leasing charges we are going to struggle to match. We're currently about €25 per week too expensive.

Todd says he's convinced that all materials and manufacturing costs have been pared back to a minimum. For instance, the diesel engine supplier has now reached their absolute limit of discount.

Sylvia has been scratching her head too. She can't move on her leasing costs (which do take account of an estimated and fairly risky residual value) but wonders why Sam insists on a 500-hour service interval on the new product.

Sam is a little surprised at this intervention and troubles himself to explain that the oil needs to be changed at that interval as recommended by the engine manufacturer otherwise their warranty terms will be breached.

Todd goes on to highlight that it would be too expensive to replace the cheap paper-based oil filter with an acceptable and fancy long-lasting neoprene-based alternative because their procurement colleagues say that would incur an unacceptable extra €2,000 to the build cost. He stresses again the manufacturing, procurement and accounts divisions' determination to cut costs to an absolute minimum.

Sylvia taps on her calculator and notices that spreading the extra €2,000 over a seven-year term is only around €5.50 per week and after deducting the attendance and materials costs of the redundant 500 hour/six monthly service regime, the projected weekly value actually matches the other supplier. She gingerly voices this to the team, to which Sam rolls his eyes.

Mike reflects and quietly mutters "you mean if we increased the selling price, we could actually save money for the Customer?". The realisation kicks in and they all sit in silence for a few minutes.

Recognising this is a pivotal point of some importance, Mike ends the meeting and asks for a review of today's findings and for further similar suggestions to be made available for their next meeting.

The team are not yet at the point of servitzation because they have not figured out how to confer outcome benefits to the airport. They are merely trying to match a contract hire price with the resident provider.

On their future journey they will be meeting even more obstacles and pivot points, and much of the rest of this book will predict and dwell on these issues.

They will come to realise that their whole machine range needs their Design Team to seek servicing efficiencies from the start

Over the coming months, Mike and his team will return with ideas that stretch the whole organisation, not just their particular development project.

They will come to realise that their whole machine range needs their design team to seek servicing efficiencies from the start. The optimal positioning of filters or filler caps, hydraulic oil level sight indicators etc are tiny things but will ensure that daily operator checks and routine servicing work will in future be designed to be a breeze, take less time and be electronically logged as a standard. They will ultimately realise that there should be no need for the airport authority to use a contract hire intermediary.

There will be a host of extra value for the team to get involved with, especially using the new telematics system, initially to just monitor the performance of their new machine, but given a short time and a good hearing they will imagine far more creative ways that an airport could use telematics information, for instance, on improving security clearances for air-side machinery service staff.

Human and equipment proximity cameras and sensors will be commonplace to guard against collision accidents – aircraft are extremely expensive to repair, humans are priceless. Near misses will be automatically recorded and reviewed.

Logging ground machinery movements that provide new streams of data about efficiencies will be received involving equipment and aircraft positioning in addition to improving machinery up-times, fuel savings and training standards of drivers.

Ultimately this will lead to consulting about replacing diesel equipment with battery or hydrogen powered alternatives, or re-engineering existing units from diesel to greener technology – all to help ensure that the airport and its stakeholders can meet their own challenging Net Zero obligations.

Mike and the team will be full of ideas. They have now named their Project as 'Plan B'. One of their biggest challenges will be to convince colleagues and senior management that their ideas should be taken seriously, not only for their own limited project but for the whole organisation too.

Developing their stakeholder management skills is crucial.

Developing their stakeholder management skills is crucial to prevent a stalling of the project. It will be key to promoting understanding and collaboration across their company and especially senior management people (see Figure 3). We will meet this topic in a variety of guises in further chapters.

These changes will demand challenging responses by way of bringing into play the multiple lessons that will develop during JENZZO's Plan B Project. We can already begin to get more than a hint about the need to draw together the 'C Suite', Management, the whole workforce, key external stakeholders, R&D, Design, Engineering,

Procurement, Manufacturing, IT, Finance, Legal, Sales, Service and Marketing to bring about an all-in philosophy that provides Advanced Services contracts for Customers. These will carry guarantees about how JENZZO's products deliver beneficial outcomes – distinctly different from mere equipment performance.

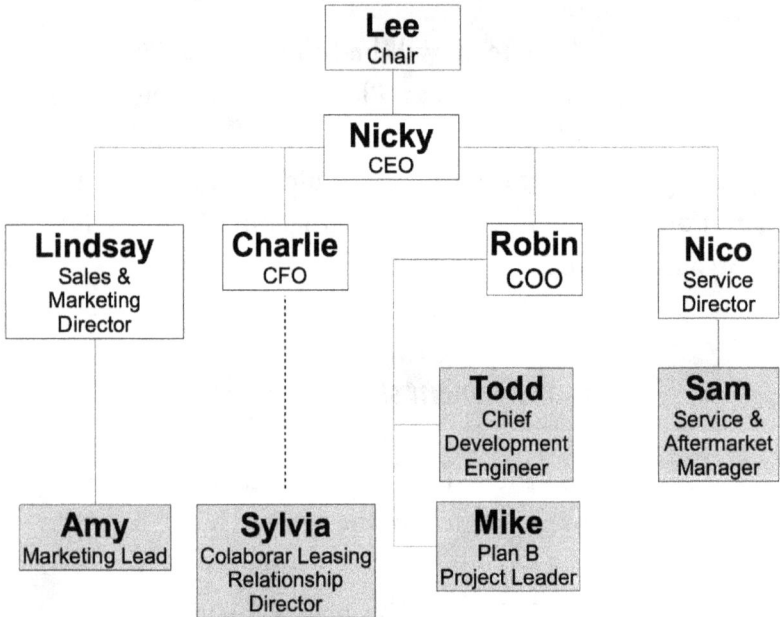

Figure 3: JENZZO Simplified Organisation Chart. (Plan B Team members in shaded boxes)

If the old days and old ways are going to have an honourable funeral for having served so well for so many years, what are the transformational plans?

We will rejoin the Plan B Team in the following chapters but leaders within JENNZO Group will have to recognise that they need to start to think urgently about WHAT, WHY, HOW & WHEN.

Summary & Resources

This brief chapter offers up a definition of Servitization and Advanced Services, and also introduces the fictitious business called JENZZO and some of its actors who will be present throughout the rest of the book.

The story catches them at a pivotal moment when the penny drops that extending their services and looking at price positioning and creating value in a different way could be a route to creating demand and combating other suppliers.

Many special projects struggle because of a lack of a shared vision and application. Effective stakeholder management will either see this through to success or lead to its stall. The Plan B Team realise they are now standing at the banks of the Rubicon.

Authoritative accounts of servitization and world class expertise, textbooks, guidebooks, and templates on the topic are available from:
https://www.advancedservicesgroup.co.uk/

[1] *Servitization & Advanced Services explained*:
https://www.advancedservicesgroup.co.uk/#:~:text=-
Explained - Servitization and Advanced Services

CHAPTER 5

The Funding Challenge

Naturally, companies tend to take a great deal of care about managing their own funding needs. The scale of financial management escalates dramatically for larger businesses and becomes astronomic with quoted companies and multi-nationals. Teams of extremely intelligent people can be engaged and led by a Chief Financial Officer (CFO) who is ultimately responsible for producing timely and reliable information for the senior management team, shareholders, investors, banks, markets and suppliers. See table below.

Selection of CFO Key Financial Performance Indicators	
EBITDA	Cash Conversion Cycle (CCC)
Return on Equity (ROE)	Debt Service Coverage
Working Capital Ratio	Return on Assets (ROA)
Debt-to-Equity Ratio	Inventory Turnover
Quick Ratio	Cash Flow

Ultimately, it's a matter of ensuring that the company is viable, trading solvently and delivering financial value to stakeholders with utmost integrity.

I had to understand this kind of financial management because of the career I chose, but it was never core to my personality. Accountancy can be a forbidding or mystifying topic to a lot of people too. I call this internal financial management and overseeing '*Finance 1*'. It is plainly crucial to the success of any business that constant professional control is exercised in this area. I'm glad that I was supported by talented people who enjoyed the topic. The type of funding I am concentrating on for most of the rest of this book will be called '*Finance 2*'.

What is Finance 2?

My avid interest here is how Customers access finance to acquire or invest in the goods sold by manufacturers. It is external to the financial management of the manufacturer and is often neglected as part of the sales process. I call it 'Finance 2'.

It's about helping the Customer to buy

It is not about the laudable husbandry of a manufacturer's financial standing and performance, it is about a manufacturer or supplier working towards delivering goods and services in the best financial and commercial interests of its Customers – it's about helping the Customer to buy through justifying and easing the cost of investment.

In many cases, manufacturers will simply leave things up to the Customer – <u>after they have committed to buy</u> – to arrange their own finance through their own banks or a basket of other leasing and asset finance companies or a multitude of commission-based credit brokers.

To my mind, that's really odd because a manufacturer usually sets out to proudly manage its brand and heritage, the spirit of excellence in the way it innovates, designs, develops and manufactures class-leading products. It goes on to market and promote these first-rate products and places its front-line sales force or a distributor's sales force at the point of sale, and then expects them to conduct and win challenging negotiations with Customers. It may even talk about its own brilliant aftercare services on offer, but how many times does a cohesively crafted proposal get left with the Customer to source a third-party bank or finance company to fund the investment? It is an all too regular gap in a manufacturer's sales process, a missing link in the chain. It gets worse – suppose the funder has a preference or a formal arrangement with another machinery supplier and immediately suggests to the Customer that an alternative proposal should be considered?

It is surely negligent to leave the funding question out of the sales process

I feel it is surely negligent to leave the funding question out of the sales process. In this day and age, salespeople should not be sent ill-equipped to close a hard-fought transaction because of a lack of knowledge or access to sales-aid finance.

Supermarket Challenge

I offer a challenge here to anyone who has decided to make a journey to acquire goods from a supermarket. Has anyone ever filled a shopping trolley and got to the checkout and said to the cashier "I'll have this trolley load of stuff but sorry – I haven't got any money"? I doubt the shopping list would have been written down at home and the car journey would not have been made without knowing in advance that access to covering the cost of the purchase was already arranged either via cash or a sales-aid debit or credit card.

This is also true in so many cases with commercial investments. At the very germ of an intention to invest, whether that has been initiated by the Customer or sparked into life by a successful call from a member of the manufacturer's Sales Team, the money issue is in the mind of the buyer and this should receive great attention in the manufacturer's sales process.

What comes first – the Money or the Machine?

We'll meet this topic again in a later chapter but for now I will leave you with another scenario. I've been present when seasoned salespeople have been asked about their successful deal closure rate compared to enquiries received. In some cases their closure rate had been 25% and on exploring the reasons why 75% of leads drifted off the radar, the most regular explanation was that the Customer bought another brand or a cheaper unit. However, delving into the facts tended to show that a high proportion of Customers hadn't bought at all.

The Customer had failed to be able to justify the investment. Some sales would have certainly been captured by other suppliers, but none of those individual suppliers matched the figure for 'NO DECISION'. There is a way to help the Customer to cost justify and we'll meet it later. It does have relevance to using finance as part of a sales negotiation, but for now we'll carry on with some descriptions and characteristics of how finance arrangements can be set up.

For instance, using an independent finance company can offer access to funds for the Customer to complete their acquisition. Some Customers may already have good relations with a finance company either directly or via a commercial finance broker, but many don't have any existing ties. There is a distinct disadvantage for the manufacturer if the funding is being treated simply as a payment method rather than an initial part of the sales process to help make an attractive offer in the first place and then use it to close a deal, hence the phrase 'What comes first, the money or the machine?'.

Taking the money with you can be quite a persuasive practice and will be covered in more detail in a later chapter.

Manufacturer-linked funding models are described below. For simplicity, for the time being, I will refer to asset finance contracts as leases. There are many other types of agreements and terminologies such as Hire Purchase (HP) or Conditional Sale, Personal Contract Purchase (PCP), Business Contract Purchase, Contract Hire, Finance Lease, Operating Lease, Re-Finance and more. The finance industry appears to like complexity! A good explanation of terminology can be found in: *A to Z of Leasing and Asset Finance* by Julian Rose & Stephen Bassett.[1]

How Does a Typical Lease Deal Work?

A simple lease structure where the manufacturer concludes a deal with the Customer is shown in the graphic. (See Figure 4)

A lease contract is arranged on the equipment with the Customer by a third-party leasing firm on a medium- to long-term basis in return for regular, usually monthly, lease repayments. The leasing company actually purchases the equipment from the manufacturer (and becomes the owner), paying in full when the equipment is delivered or installed and commissioned, allowing the manufacturer to book the sale and account for the revenue.

The repayments due to the leasing company can be collected by automated payment systems directly from the Customer's bank account. At the end of the lease, the equipment is routinely returned to the leasing company for disposal.

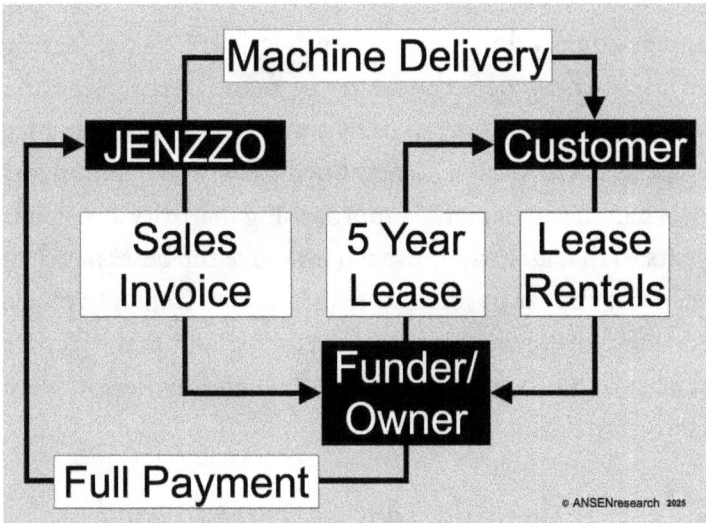

Figure 4: Structure of a Typical lease

Leasing in Practice

It is inescapable nowadays that buying a motor car is usually accompanied by an integrated finance offer, based perhaps on an attractive weekly or monthly rental or interest-free promotion that eases the buying process for the potential consumer or business purchaser. This is achieved by linking the fundamentals of assessing availability, desirability and affordability designed to convert the Customer to commit to buy. I call this 'lubrication' of a transaction. The integrated offer is not merely a purchasing option for those poor unfortunates who don't have the cash stashed under the bed mattress, it is a deal attractor and closing tool.

It is also noticeable that the finance 'deal' acts as a platform for marketing, up-selling, cross-selling and bundling service plans, insurance, other warranties and residual values. Subsequent vigilance by the leasing company may alert the dealer or manufacturer about a Customer's intention to early settle/terminate a finance agreement (a signal that a new buying decision is imminent) or when the agreement is approaching maturity at say four years so that an early approach may give the best chance of securing repeat business and aid the replacement vehicle forward-order process, procurement, and manufacture scheduling processes including the funding period from factory to dealer.

> *Grasping this concept is an early and vital enabling step to make on the journey towards Servitization*

In this way, the leasing transaction is a platform for wider adoption of services. When deploying Customer financing options, the sale can seem to be *never truly over* because methodical and important contact is maintained with the Customer years after the original sale. Grasping this concept is an early and vital enabling step to make on the journey towards Servitization – to Cross the Rubicon.

Sales-Aid Funding Model Options

There are several asset finance models used by enlightened manufacturers to lubricate Customer transactions. By this I mean having funding present at the start of negotiations that can take away friction from one of the main objections to opening and concluding a deal. It helps overcome the Customer's predictable and classic dilemma or stalling tactic of saying "er, this all sounds good but I don't have the money" or "I can't justify the outlay at the moment – send me a quote and I'll think about it". This frequently equals death of a deal.

Finance 2 Staircase

The 'Finance 2 Staircase' (see Figure 5) represents the various options available to manufacturers when seeking a funding route for their Customers.

Step 1 - As mentioned earlier, a manufacturer can abdicate from (or not even consider) how the Customer will fund their investment, leaving things entirely out of control.

Step 2 - A simple recommendation to a known leasing broker or funder is a good start but can cause issues around speed of decision, dedication, confidentiality, consistency of service, or access to competitive rates of interest.

Both of these models are not the best way of providing a sales-aid service in my opinion.

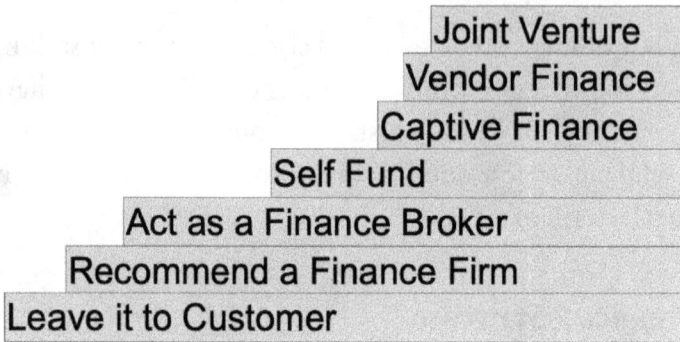

Figure 5: Finance 2 Staircase

Act as Finance Broker

Step 2 – A manufacturer may see the benefit of including a funding offer within their sales process by means of acting as a finance broker, engaged with one or more finance companies to whom leasing proposals can be made. A properly declared commission may be available for the introduction. This option is at least another move up the staircase but could involve releasing important information to third parties and be reliant on the speed at which various finance companies may respond. The lease agreement and other correspondence will not bear the manufacturer's branding and future tracking of repayments etc is not normally possible. These arrangements can work but are not as cohesive as options further up the staircase.

Self-Funding Model

Some manufacturers have sufficient financial resources to create their own relatively informal leases and provide the funds internally. They become lenders of money, although if volumes escalate, the resources and cash committed can become serious sums. Their balance sheet can begin to get loaded and lopsided with funds tied up with their own leases. The amount of administration and regulatory processes can be most burdensome and so this model can sometimes offer a temporary harbour for leases until they are sold on to a bank or other funder. This method has to contain enough return for the funder to have the appetite to take on the debt and accompanying credit risk of the Customer. The manufacturer may be required to offer the funder some kind of warranty if things go wrong, creating a contingent liability on the manufacturer's balance sheet in respect of the value of such a warranty. The manufacturer may decide to guarantee a residual value of the equipment and expect return of the goods at the end of the lease term. This has the effect of making the Customer's regular lease rentals lower. It is likely that the lease documentation and ongoing correspondence is less sophisticated than the next option.

Captive Finance

This option is similar to self-funding but involves the manufacturer setting up its own professionally branded asset finance operation and uses its own cash resources to fund Customer purchases via a lease. The administration task including eg regulatory and anti-money laundering compliance and credit risk is taken initially by the manufacturer. If the Customer does not pay money back on time or fails completely a loss could ensue. Without the Customer's knowledge, the manufacturer may routinely sell batches of the lease contracts to specialist funders who will pay funds to the manufacturer in a lump sum immediately. Again, the bundled leases must carry sufficient return for funders, often acting as syndicates, to provide them with a satisfactory margin. There could still be recourse terms meaning that the manufacture may warrant the quality of the lease portfolio sold and suffer penalties if the funder experiences poor performance of the leases.

If the debt relating to leases is not sold to an external funder, it will remain on the manufacturer's balance sheet and again skew many of the manufacturer's key ratios that are monitored intensely by the CFO and the internal Finance 1 Team. This also applies to residual value guarantees and any other form of recourse granted to the ultimate funder by the manufacturer. Regulatory compliance requirements can make this model risky and expensive for the manufacturer. An advantage is that the Customer simply sees the manufacturer's brand throughout their relationship and lease term, and it is generally the manufacturer's sales and admin staff who arrange and maintain the lease with the Customer.

Vendor Finance (VF)

This is a widely used arrangement where a manufacturer and a funder see sufficient potential new business flows to operate together in a formal way. By way of examples, in 1998 I set up vendor arrangements with Atlas Copco UK (a Swedish-based multinational supplier of compressed air solutions) and UpRight UK (a UK-based mobile access equipment distributor for UpRight Inc based in California). The manufacturer relies on the money (treasury), processes and back-office systems of the funder. These include full administration of the lease from the moment of the Customer's initial application, onto credit assessment and regulatory compliance, credit granting and credit risk and defaults handling through to the end of the lease term.

Some VF funders use this model as their standard route to market and may operate similar arrangements for several manufacturers, sometimes even competing brands. The Customer usually only sees the manufacturer's branding and the funder remains in the background.

In general terms the manufacturer has handed over the debt amount to the VF partner and such amounts will not show on the manufacturer's balance sheet. The CFO and the Finance 1 Team should be happy unless other recourse guarantees have been given to make sales happen that will find their way back onto their balance sheet.

The benefit to the manufacturer is that Customers who are considering acquiring their products can be persuaded by the sheer convenience, slickness and brand trust to take up a lease and choose their equipment. Special branded leasing offers can be projected out to the marketplace.

The cost of the funding from the VF partner will be fairly fixed, and there will be an element of premium to pay for the service provided. The manufacturer may need to support the end offer to the Customer by paying 'subsidies' to the funder, otherwise its offers could sometimes be above rates available in the general asset finance market.

Joint Venture (JV)

This is a fairly rare option. A manufacturer and a funder (likely to be a bank) agree to run a finance company together. The bank usually holds the majority share-holding. In the graphic (see Figure 6) we see a 75%/25% example. The bank will want ultimate control because it will be providing the funds to the JV. The relationship will be documented within a JV Agreement that will, for instance, record important formal rights about who can do what within operational activities, the support available from both parents (eg HR function, marketing resources), any management fees and the cost of funds attached to the money that the bank will lend to this JV entity. Again, the Customer will usually only see the manufacturer's brand.

This model creates a very focussed entity which is completely dedicated to the needs of the manufacturer's Customers. Its services perform the new business 'lubrication' role. The JV will likely be managed by its own CEO and an Executive Team, carry its own profit and loss account, and be subject to regular reviews by a formal Board. The market Regulator will take an interest in the JV Executive Team's performance and capabilities.

Interestingly, the lending balances and residual value amounts built up by the JV will not appear on the manufacturer's balance sheet because the JV is regarded as

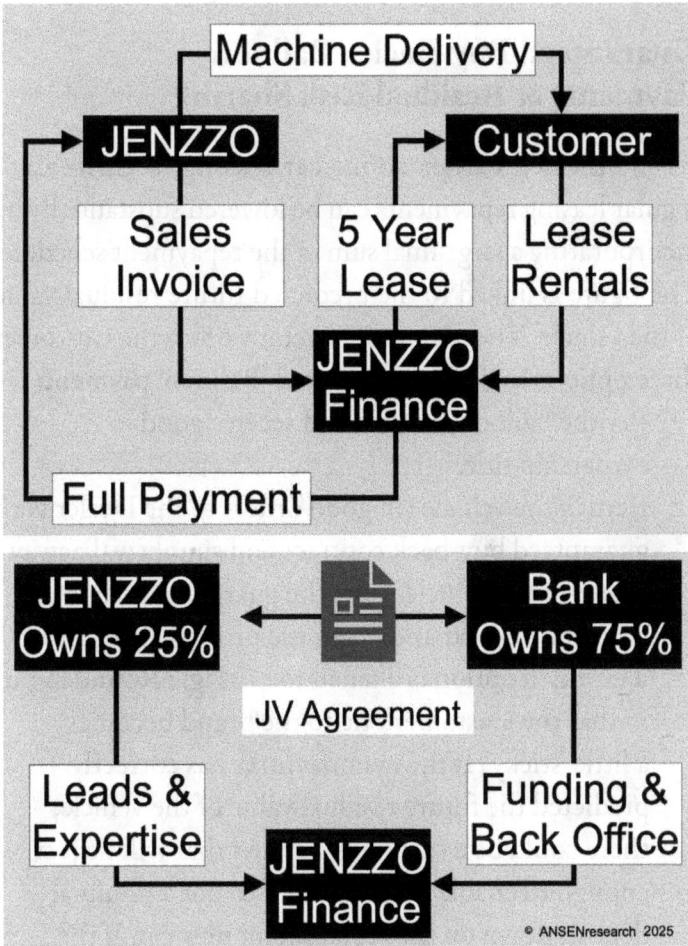

Figure 6: Simple JV Set Up

a subsidiary of the Bank, which allows the manufacturer to book a clean sale upon delivery/commissioning of the equipment. The JV can either use the back-office of the Bank or go on to create its own systems and processes under close supervision.

Guaranteed Buy-Backs, Balloon Payments & Residual Risk Sharing

As mentioned earlier about car leasing, a Customer's regular leasing repayments can be lowered substantially by incorporating a large final sum in the repayment schedule. The figure is linked to the predicted future residual value of the vehicle. The car sector generally offers the Customer three options to deal with the final 'Balloon' payment:

- Pay the balloon amount and receive good ownership title.
- Return the vehicle (in good order) to the Dealer via a guaranteed buy-back contract and simply walk away.
- Trade-in the vehicle using the guaranteed buy-back against a new car and begin the process again.
- This third option is likened to a 'Magic Roundabout' in that the Customer's tie to the brand becomes a little 'sticky'. If the manufacturer has correctly predicted the future residual value of the vehicle, there could be a surplus generated that will be just enough to enable the Customer to put a minimal deposit down on the replacement new car. If the manufacturer's predictions have not been fulfilled, trouble and losses can be expected unless the Customer can be convinced to extend the lease until car market values improve.

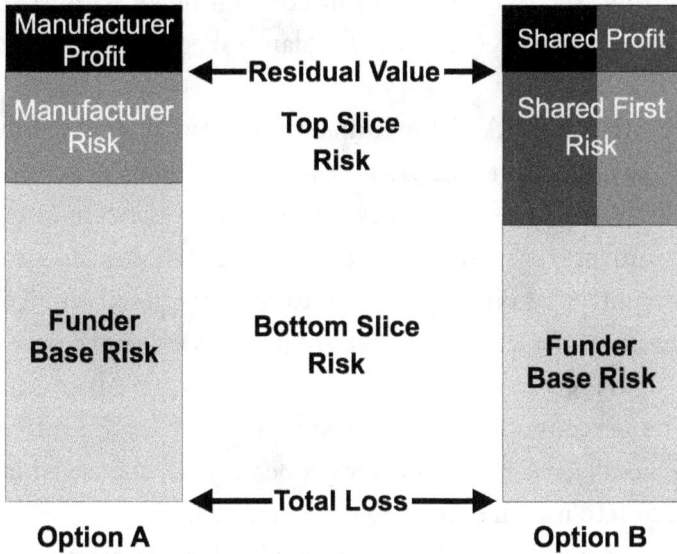

Figure 7: Residual Risk Share Example

The advent of disruptive car technology such as full battery electric, hybrid and autonomous variations, and their accompanying higher initial costs plus the emerging net zero regulatory environment and new market entrants is creating some extra and unknown challenges and questions for manufacturers and leasing companies. It is not clear how this will all shake down in the coming years. Risks are on the rise.

I've mentioned balloon payments and guaranteed buy-backs. There is another method of dealing with Residual Values and that is by means of a 'Residual Risk Share'.

There are many flavours of Residual Risk sharing where a large final repayment is built into the lease payment schedule. The examples shown in Figure 7 provide two options to reduce the quantum of contingent liability on a manufacturer's (or dealer's) balance sheet down to a first loss liability.

In Option 'A' the manufacturer provides a First Loss undertaking but receives access to 100% of any profit on re-sale. Option 'B' reduces the potential quantum of the manufacturer's loss because the Funder shares the same percentage of First Loss down to the pre-agreed set level, but in return for the Funder's higher risk exposure, access is provided to share in the potential profit on re-sale. The percentage of shared first loss/profit can be varied. Generally, the manufacturer (or dealer) can choose which option to use on each individual transaction.

Adoption of Risk Sharing could be beneficial for newly launched equipment where no reliable RV is known yet.

Recurring Revenue Financing – Finance 3

A new generation of funding has emerged recently based on monthly or annual recurring revenue financing (RRF)[2]. I'm calling it 'Finance 3'.

RRF has been primarily aimed at Technology or Software-as-a-Service subscription businesses. It has been seen as particularly useful to new start businesses that have low capital but high growth potential, and has helped entrepreneurs to retain ownership of such businesses without diluting their shareholdings.

Such funding techniques are beginning to find traction in industrial applications and a number of specialist firms have sprung up to provide manufacturers with XaaS funding solutions often coupled with repair and maintenance contracts and advanced services. A main consideration for accounting treatment is whether the debt involved actually sits off-balance sheet for the manufacturer or the user or both. RRF derivatives may offer workable solutions to manufacturers and Customers to handle this.

Growth of these firms is taking place, sometimes working with significant names within the manufacturing sector.

The term 'Industrial Internet of Things' (IIOT) has been coined to distinguish matters away from consumer and pure technology dealings.

Summary & Resources

This chapter is called the 'Funding Challenge' for several reasons which manufacturers should consider carefully:

- If not already in place, does the firm recognise the benefits of adopting a sales-aid asset finance solution for Customers?
- If this is adopted, remembering that the CFO and Finance 1 Team function is mostly internally facing, where should reporting lines sit within the manufacturer?
- Which model should be explored and adopted, including recurring revenue financing?
- What extra skills and resources are required and what benefits should be seen?
- What risks are there in adopting this <u>or not adopting it?</u>
- How does adoption aid the route to improving provision of bundled services?
- What does best in class look like?

Finance and Leasing Association, London
https://fla.org.uk/

Leaseurope, Brussels, Belgium
https://www.leaseurope.org/about-us

[1] *A to Z of Leasing and Asset Finance*
Julian Rose & Stephen Bassett. UK Book Publishing.
ISBN: 9781917329293

[2] *Recurring Revenue Financing: An Increasingly Popular Option - Lucosky Brookman*
https://www.lucbro.com/news/blogs/detail/10541/
recurring-revenue-financing-an-increasingly-popular-option

CHAPTER 6

Business Transformation

There are countless books and experts on business transformation. Some are terrific and some are not grounded in practical reality. I remember reading a scholarly management tome back in 2003 about the brilliance and sheer audacity of the Royal Bank of Scotland's (RBS) takeover of the much larger NatWest Bank. The book went on to extol the virtues of dynamism and strong leadership that ultimately created an international behemoth which became one of the world's largest banking groups. Of course, RBS failed miserably in 2008 and nearly blew up the UK's economy.

Many banking governance and business lessons were learnt as a result of this national disaster. A great number of people endured hardship in the aftermath including taxpayers, shareholders, Customers and long-term employees of RBS and NatWest, many of whom lost their life savings that were tied up in share-save schemes that had been encouraged by senior management.

The next part of this book looks at transforming a business to strengthen its defences against low-cost imports, particularly in the light of the Net Zero paradox. It is based on my own experience and is not drawn heavily on scholarly or orthodox material.

...you probably rely on people and the agendas and beliefs that they each hold!

Unless you have a fully robotic production capability plus AI enabled design, on-line sales & distribution and service functions, you will probably rely on people and the agendas and beliefs that they each hold!

For this purpose, from time to time, we will again be watching developments through the eyes of Mike, Todd, Sam, Amy and Sylvia at JENZZO as they build bonds between each other and wider patronage with their own stakeholders for their project (now called 'Plan B') and come to realise that their actions and ideas have enormous consequences for the company rather than just for one new product line.

During my managerial time I relied a lot on a quote I heard on UK national radio. It was a BBC interview aired with Lord Hanson shortly before his death in 2004. He was a UK industrialist who built a very large group called Hanson PLC. He achieved this alongside his friend and Finance Director, Lord White. They pursued a formula based on leveraged buyouts. The approach often fell into the 'asset stripping' category by locating and purchasing under-managed businesses in quite diverse sectors, then wringing out inefficiencies and generating cash, which often meant making people redundant.

The negative qualities of his approach to business were not what attracted me! His radio quote came over the airwaves while I was driving to an appointment and it went something like this:

"I was just an ordinary chap, born in Huddersfield, but I found that I had a good understanding of human behaviour. I practised three things:

- **"Give meaning and purpose to people in their working lives."**
- **"Enforce high esteem amongst a team."**
- **"Add a little pressure into the system."**

This quote, in isolation from Hanson's reputation, became a guiding insight for the rest of my career.

A second driver for me, even as a CEO, was that I saw bottom line profit as the by-product of what we were there to do. If we served the Customers properly, based on a firm set of values, with the financial products that provided the best outcomes for their success, then our business would flourish, which it did.

A third insight was provided by a senior director within the banking sector who told me that in a mature business within a mature market, if we needed to change, we had to:

- **"Cause a bit of chaos"** and
- **"Change the people or change the people".**

I found out that this is not easy and requires lots of resilience, care and tenacity. I also kept in mind the anecdote about the life of a special project, especially the final sentence!

Reaction to Change

In the words of Zig Ziglar, *"Your life does not get better by chance, it gets better by change"*. In business, crossing the Rubicon from one state to another can be a fairly bumpy process. There are many depictions of how people react to change. I've been through many changes during my career and have embraced most of them with enthusiasm, but when threatened, there are common reactions that follow a timeline such as:

- **Normality** - Disrupted because a major change is announced
- **Shock and Worry** - Do I lose my job, money, friends, status?
- **Disbelief** - Why would 'they' do this to me/us?
- **Resist** - We don't deserve this. Attempt to build coalitions against the change.
- **Negotiate** - Minimise impact on self. Obfuscate in an attempt to thwart change.
- **Debilitation** - Shock shatters self-worth and creates feelings of powerlessness.
- **Letting Go** - Realisation that the change is definite and fighting may harm future prospects within the new order.
- **Collaborate with the Inevitable** - Final

acceptance and switch to optimising self-interests within new order.

I did have some low points and have felt loneliness when stability, self-worth and the future have seemed uncertain or threatened. But gradually, sometimes reluctantly, I accepted the new status quo which worked out okay in the longer term. More often I usually thrived in a constantly changing environment.

Communication

Communication from management during important change is absolutely essential to prevent rumour filling the void. My favourite phrase for this is "have you heard the rumour about poor communication?".

> *"Have you heard the rumour about poor communication?"*

The best change environment is where a business wants to excel and be a pace-setter that gives hope and expectation to everyone involved that tomorrow will be more rewarding and more secure than today. Too many businesses feel the pressure of pursuing financial targets at the expense of neglecting their raison d'être. Phrases like we need to 'cut our way to glory' should be binned.

Building an Exceptional Team

Without an exceptional team, successful business transformation can be very difficult. There are huge numbers of books, self-help programmes, competency analyses, videos and consultants that provide guidance, hints and tips that can help form exceptional performance in a team. I've encountered many. Some have been a revelation, some have seemed to make good sense, some threatening, some a waste of time and money.

> *Without an exceptional team, successful business transformation can be very difficult.*

Analysis of some individual characteristics can be very helpful, not only to leaders who wish to build and maintain an exceptional team but also to the team members themselves.

Moulding the Team

So how about moulding an exceptional team? As a Manager, I'd firstly consider the 'Enthusiasm and Ability' matrix. (See Figure 8)

- The **Champion** will excel at most things and is probably good at sport too. The irony is that sometimes they don't make good leaders and can occasionally have narcissistic traits that need moderating (they won't shake off the trait).
-

- The idea is to train and show faith in the **Followers** to gain ability.
- The **Coaster** needs motivating to exhibit more enthusiasm although this is more difficult than attending to the Follower.
- As for the **Drainer**, they tend to be cynical detractors and may show disdain for almost anything that crosses their path. The tactic here is to be honest and confront the shortcoming with a view to releasing them from their tiresome duties and, importantly, be seen by the rest of the team to do so.

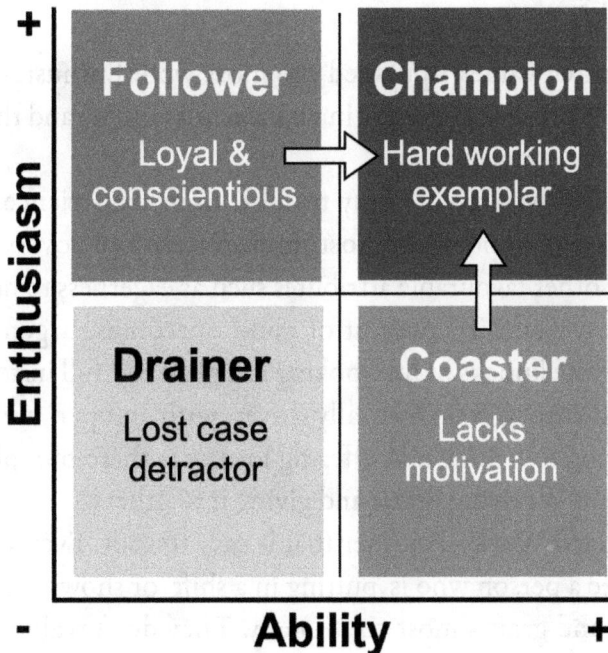

Figure 8: Enthusiasm and Ability Matrix

71

Creating elitism in the Champion and their new acolytes should be avoided as it can cause resentment and be self-defeating within the wider organisation.

The Manager also has a challenge in creating desire in their wider stakeholders to support the transformation in the first place. There could be many stakeholders – influencing and persuading colleagues to move in a new direction opens up many challenges requiring diplomacy, guile, advocacy and marshalling allies while deploying strong and effective human relations skills. Part of the task is called 'cross-cutting'. We will look at that shortly.

Values

The three values I pursued the most were Enthusiasm, Hard Work and Honesty (in no particular order) and they are inter-connected.

Enthusiasm - It's easy to spot. In my experience, it shines out of people almost immediately and covers so many other favourable attributes such as eagerness to take on responsibility, pursuit of good outcomes, urgency, riding the knocks of life, looking at a glass half full instead of half empty. It is internally driven with an open mind. Wanting to belong and offering loyalty is there too, plus enjoying receiving praise and giving it to others.

Hard Work - Another that is easy to spot. Everyone can see a person who is 'putting in a shift' or showing real drive and graft almost continually. They don't walk past a problem and are suckers to solve the difficult issues, especially when the chips are down. They get results about the right issues and remain tenaciously focussed on the right outcomes.

Honesty - This attribute means that people will not let others down. They wouldn't do something their mother wouldn't like. Not because she's always watching, but because it just isn't within them anyway.

Enthusiasm and hard work can be a little flexible. No-one can give 110% all the time and no-one should expect that they can. On the other hand, honesty is not a two strikes and you're out situation – you are out at the first strike. It's brittle and fragile. If honesty was a china plate, it would smash the first time it hit the floor.

Honest mistakes do happen and these have to be fessed up straight away, even big ones. Sympathy and corrective action can create long term loyalty.

Plan B Project Team Update

At this stage, let's cut back to Mike and the team and their 'Plan B' task to 'Pivot to Providing Services'. We last met them in Chapter Four where they were on the verge of realising that there were many more benefits to adopting Servitization than they first imagined.

Their task to influence stakeholders has grown by quite a factor. They now appreciate that they have a tiger by the tail. The project has evolved beyond introducing a new aircraft tug entering a mature and competitive market, into persuading JENZZO Group to adopt what they are proposing within their Plan B project. There are a host of benefits that the Customer can receive if products are aligned to outcomes rather than simply paying to acquire products to do a job.

Mike has been taking advice from his boss, CEO Nicky, who has suggested that the Plan B Team take some time out on an away-day to get to build a stronger team ethic between the members.

Nicky understood that it would be ideal to staff the project with exceptional performers but, as is so often the case, compromises have to be made. Not every 'top performer' can be allocated to a difficult project and furthermore, assembling a team from 'Alpha' characters can cause difficulties too. Nicky was content that that the team members would have sufficient capacity to avoid the risk of gaps and provide timely solutions.

This resulted in an off-site session facilitated by a team-building consultant who introduced Mike, Todd, Sam, Amy and Sylvia to a number of competency and self-discovery tools to uncover the inventory of skills they possess. The tools included:

- **360o Feedback** - Personal critique in a safe space.
- **Belbin Team Inventory**[1] - Identifies behavioural strengths and weaknesses in the workplace.
- **Myers Briggs Self Awareness Test**[2] - To help people identify and gain some understanding around how they take in information and make decisions, the patterns of perception and judgment, as seen in normal, healthy behaviour.
- **Johari Window Test**[3] - Helps to understand the differences between how people see us and how we see ourselves. The test can uncover personal

blind spots.
* **Strength Deployment Inventory (SDI)**[4] - To identify strengths, overdone strengths and conflict style and how to improve relationships at work.

We now catch up with the Plan B Team on another regular session. They learnt a lot about each other and themselves during their away-day and their new bonds are playing an important part in maintaining focus, trust, resilience and momentum in the project and wider ambition.

JENZZO Plan B Away-Day Results

The away-day was a success and each team member felt that being open during the various character exercises and receiving 360° feedback cemented their bonds. Mike's leadership was strengthened. Todd's grasp of the future challenges facing the Design and Engineering Team was much clearer, he felt that he could challenge pre-conceptions that had been around for years. Sam had learned a lot about his interpersonal skills and made a commitment to be less abrasive about suggestions from colleagues who he had considered were junior to his position. He recognised the significance of what the project team were involved in and committed himself to raise his game and become 'smarter'. Amy grew in confidence and felt that Mike's support would go a long way when called upon. Sylvia now felt immersed and welcome within JENZZO and realised she had a big part to play in the coming weeks and months.

They set to work on a cross-cutting matrix (see Figure 9) so that the Plan B Team could figure out who they needed to influence and who would do the influencing of the stakeholders they have been allocated.

	ExCo	Management Team	Accounts & Legal	HR	R&D/Design	Procurement	Manufacturing	Service & Parts	Sales/Marketing/ Distribution	Distributors
Nicky - Mike's Boss	✓	✓		✓						✓
Mike - Project Leader	✓	✓	✓	✓				✓	✓	✓
Todd - Chief Development Engineer					✓	✓	✓			
Sam - Service & Aftermarket				✓				✓		✓
Amy - Marketing Lead								✓	✓	✓
Sylvia - Leasing Partner	✓	✓	✓		✓			✓	✓	✓

Figure 9: Cross Cutting Matrix

Mike was relying on his boss, Nicky, to support the cross-cutting work so that collaboration could be free of excessive friction. Each member of the team now had to focus on selected areas across the company's operations. To help with this, regular reviews with senior managers were to be arranged by Nicky to prepare the ground for important decisions.

As part of that task each separate JENZZO department was assessed in terms of their power and interest in the progress of Plan B. They put together a useful Power vs Interest matrix (see Figure 10). It was noted that the participants and their segment position could change during the life of the project.

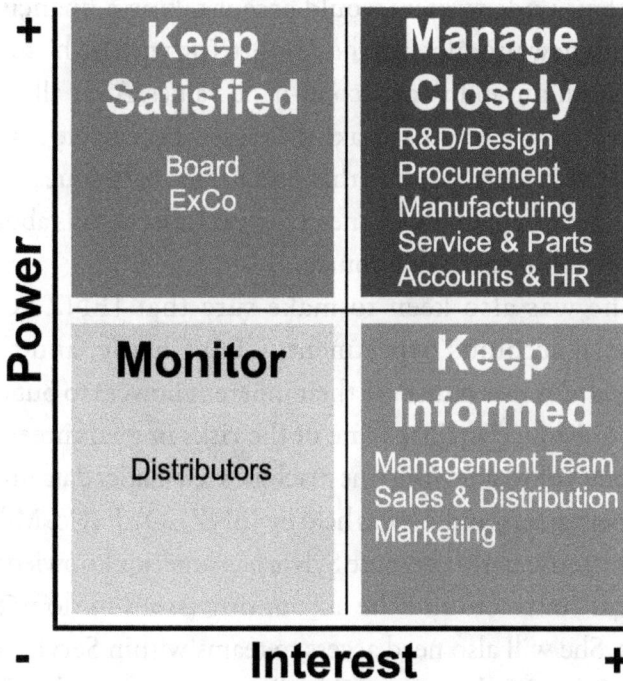

Figure 10: Power Versus Interest Matrix

Each person seemed content with their task although Mike was surprised at the level of access and responsibility that the Plan B Team had allocated to Sylvia (from their independent leasing partner, C Leasing). Although Mike and the rest of the team rated Sylvia's credentials, he asked her to arrange and did obtain a Non-Disclosure Agreement (NDA) signed by a Bank director to ensure confidentiality of her work. She saw this as standard commercial practice.

They had a private chat later and Amy explained that she needed to give maximum confidence to her stakeholders back at C Leasing if she was going to stand a good chance that their underwriters would accept taking a financing risk on a new product like the Airport Tug with no historic data about durability or second-hand values. After all, the residual value levels that make the transaction viable in the market are a best guess at this point. Her colleagues and senior management would need to hear fuller details about Plan B ambitions in due course.

She was also keen to make sure that JENZZO's financial accounts department, CFO Charlie, and the Internal Counsel didn't use their inherent powers to put up early resistance against some of the risks in guaranteeing Customer outcomes from the machine's telematics data until a deeper understanding was held by JENZZO's ExCo. Mike saw the sense in this because Sylvia has superior knowledge of legal contracts and the accounting issues to do with leases. She will also need access to teams within Service & Parts, Sales, Marketing and Distribution to ensure that the extensive bundled contract she is co-drafting will include the terms and conditions required by all parties. This will need to be understood by the Sales and Marketing Team for targeting and promotion campaigns, and she and her colleagues already deal extensively with people involved in Distribution and Dealer networks.

Amy was charged with creating an internal campaign to build understanding and support for the project and thwart some of the 'Drainers' or detractors. The campaign would also prime selected department heads to become involved in brainstorming sessions to help burst through complicated issues and achieve faster progress.

Preparing JENZZO for Servitization Transformation

The Plan B Team now feel they're well on the way to building in-depth collaboration with colleagues on accepting a new form of trading on the Airport Tug and using it to spearhead a servitization transformation journey throughout the JENZZO Group.

As we see later, there will be bumps in the road because the Plan B Team will learn quickly and be testing their innovative ideas and be making some serious requests for change. The introduction of a 24/48 hour key decision standard was an important move to enable progress blocks to be removed so that progress remained on track. They will ultimately be looking at things like multiple profit centres, design for outcomes, open Customer systems and data driven decisions, all of which impact every team and process in the business. The challenges they face will escalate and need careful management and support.

Let's take a look at some of the early realisations of the Project B Team:

Multiple Profit Centres

JENZZO Group is structured into distinct Divisions or Key Business Units (KBU) to aid focus on specific parts of the firm. For instance, the Ports Handling Division, Rail Logistics Division, Waste Recovery Division and Municipal Equipment Division. Some sub-assemblies are made in-house by the Components Division. There is a Service & Parts Division and a sub-Division producing accessories, internally called 'Hobart's Funnies' after the British wartime inventor.

Alongside these Divisions is the network of seven regional offices and teams representing JENZZO worldwide.

Each Division carries its own budget with its attendant Profit & Loss (P&L) account. There are serious repercussions if Divisional Heads miss their P&L targets which screw up the CFO's group numbers. However, over the years, this arrangement has been mostly successful in driving the three metrics of: quality, growth, cost (and personal standing/promotion of Divisional Heads!).

The system does have its drawbacks by sometimes creating friction over who gets priority of support from centralised functions such as Procurement, Sales & Marketing and Central Finance for product development funding. There was at least one occasion when procurement were by-passed and the Group ended up with three different suppliers of identical components all at different prices!

Over time, the Service Division has become a flagship for profitability

Over time, the Service Division has become a flagship for profitability. Margins in the aftermarket are very high, and much effort has been put in to ensure Customers come back for genuine replacement parts. Paradoxically, this can lead to a problem.

Each Division will naturally be protective of their P&L performance even though this arrangement contributes to added cost throughout the price build-up. This also extends externally to the margins vigorously protected by C Leasing.

The servitization transformation will need to trample over these 'Fiefdoms' or silos and involve end-to-end thinking and responsibility to the point that the equipment sale may not generate its customary overall contribution. Remembering that the Rolls-Royce 'Power by the Hour' model is renowned for almost disregarding the capital sale profit of a high value aero engine for the sake of it creating a far bigger long term income platform from the service provided during its whole working life.

This does not bode well for a business that is trapped in providing quarterly reports to shareholders and the market, given that short-term profits will inevitably drop during the transition phase to a longer-term business model. We will see later that Mike and his Plan B Team realise they have another 'Tiger by the Tail' here.

Design for Outcomes

We saw a glimpse of this earlier when it was realised that fitting a more expensive part actually reduced the overall Customer price of the advanced services contract on the Airport Tug.

Product design for outcomes means focusing on the results or impact of a product, rather than solely on its features or appearance. This approach involves designing products that are intended to change both JENZZO and Customer behaviour, achieve specific business goals, and deliver tangible value. It emphasises understanding the user's needs, the desired outcomes, and designing solutions that effectively address those needs and achieve the desired results.

The Customer is therefore paying for solutions or guaranteed outcomes. JENZZO will begin to be responsible for costs and risks that were previously in the Customer's domain after the sale had been cleanly executed. I call the old method 'Fire and Forget', ie the Sales Team fire the missile at the target and move on to the next deal, followed by the Service Division who pick up the relationship from that point and have to deal with warranty issues, servicing and parts needs and even poorly thought out equipment specifications that turn out not to be fit for purpose. In an outcome-based world the Customer is not interested in any gap between Divisions but is required to recognise the transfer of risks involved and financially compensate for it.

I've always been perplexed as to why a supplier would ask a Customer to sign up to a wordy extended warranty contract if the Customer has entered a bundled leased product that includes a priced-up full service, repair and maintenance for the duration of the contract. In the Customer's eyes (product abuse aside), it should be said that "if the equipment breaks down, I've paid for you to come and fix it, extended warranty is irrelevant". Extended warranty is reflective of a poor organisational interpretation of what has happened and is merely an internal paperwork exercise that follows a process that assumes a legacy cash sale. It should have no place in a guaranteed outcomes world.

Customers invest in new equipment or systems for only two reasons: either to make more money or to save money.

Similarly, within servitization, the costs of servicing and purchase of replacement parts or the actual durability or suitability of the equipment is no longer a Customer issue. The manufacturer is now feeling those Customer pain points like never before and this can be the quickest way to improve design, engineering integrity and service capability.

The transformed design philosophy has to incorporate some important considerations such as:

- **Outcomes vs Outputs** - The prime focus is away from features and benefits to achieving what the Customer wants and expects. The expectations may soon involve novel requirements not entirely based on traditional outputs especially in relation to aiding the Customer to meet their own Net Zero targets.

- **User Behaviours** - This requires designers to prioritise understanding the Customer's needs and designing solutions that nudge specific interactions with products that lead to those desired outcomes.
- **Business Goals** - In my experience, Customers invest in new equipment or systems for only two reasons – either to make more money or to save money. This may involve more considerations as Net Zero targets begin to drive novel goals, but money will still remain at the centre.
- **Measurable Results** - Outcome-focused design emphasises defining and measuring the impact of the product, allowing for data-driven decision-making.
- **Improved User Experience:** By focusing on user needs and desired outcomes, products are more likely to be intuitive, user-friendly, and effective in achieving the user's goals.
- **Increased Business Value:** Outcome-focused design can drive more meaningful business results by ensuring that products address key needs and achieve desired outcomes.
- **Reduced Development Costs:** By focusing on outcomes early in the design process, teams can avoid building unnecessary features or solutions that don't contribute to the desired results, potentially saving time, cost and resources.
- **Data-Driven Decision Making:** Outcome-focused design allows for more accurate measurement of success, enabling data-driven decision-making and continuous improvement.

HR Understanding – A Key Enabler

Just as the Plan B Team had undergone some self-discovery during their away-day, the Team recognised that their task could not be progressed without creating a deep understanding with their HR Team and their resources and influence. Reorientation of mindsets would be key to success in the business transformation quest. Much time and effort would be spent with the HR Team to ensure that they grasped the fundamentals of what was to come in terms of reshaping job profiles, redesigning competencies and capabilities and a thorough redefining of performance reviews and incentive programmes. The HR Team reported to the CFO and it was vital to ensure that Charlie bought into the intensity of the change management process required to shift JENZZO from the time honoured, almost revered, 'cash' sales and aftermarket trading model to launching advanced services – and make it a success.

Work would soon begin on a companywide capability and competency audit. Creating understanding and providing training and coaching would be prime elements and tackle employees believing 'it's not my problem'. Fortunately, Charlie was impressed enough with the thoroughness of the Team's deliberations and wanted to play a low-key part in the transition, albeit for now. The sudden shake up in the longstanding global trading terms and increased threat from low-cost suppliers had begun to sink in. Using foresight, it was also fairly obvious to involve some outside help that would be needed to aid the transition. The HR Team were on the case.

New job profiles would be drawn up to cover such issues as capabilities, systems, knowledge and agility. The idea of moving from up-front € values to achieving and monitoring Customer satisfaction sounded a tough, rather nebulous task to begin with, but it was agreed that doing the tough thing was doing the right thing. In due course, they would have to find a way to assess behaviours beyond immediate financial hard results.

At this stage, Charlie felt it was pragmatic and politically expedient to be seen to play a part.

Summary & Resources

We've heard about a comprehensive set of actions and intentions to effect a successful business transition. A high degree of attention has been aimed at people, either persuading key stakeholders to buy into ideas or making preparations to influence a wider acceptance of change that is on the near horizon. Actions have been thorough although fairly conventional.

A lot has been considered in a short space of time and that has been in tune with the urgency required to secure JENZZO's prospects in the rapidly changing business environment.

Plan B Leader Mike was shrewd enough to pick up on Charlie's somewhat ambivalent stance and began to wonder if the paradigm had truly shifted or was there room yet for a stall at a later stage?

[1] *Belbin Team Inventory*
https://www.belbin.com/about/belbin-team-roles

[2] *Myers Briggs Self Awareness Test*
https://www.themyersbriggs.com/en-US/
Products-and-Services/Myers-Briggs

[3] *Johari Window Test*
https://en.wikipedia.org/wiki/Johari_window

[4] *Strength Deployment Inventory (SDI)*
https://beyondtheory.co.uk/
personality-profiling-strength-deployment-inventory

CHAPTER 7

The Rubicon Performance Leap

L et's carry on with a little bit more fiction within JENZZO Group. A few weeks ago, Lindsay had risen up through the ranks and was appointed as Sales Director. The first experience of an annual budgeting meeting was about to happen with a group of senior management including the CEO Nicky, CFO Charlie and COO Robin. It's a ritual that most senior salespeople go through at least once a year where they're directly challenged to make the company's numbers work.

A study of performance over the past few years, showed that the net profit had become fairly static. Their Chairperson, Lee, had been to visit and stated that the business had stagnated which left senior people feeling a bit raw. Lindsay knew that being appointed as Sales Director was a direct result of that rebuke and could expect to be charged with doing something about it.

The traditional gambit from the CFO was to announce

what was perceived as the minimum that the shareholders would accept as EBITDA, PBT, ROE, costs, head count etc. This year, Lindsay had heard that budgeted Profit Before Tax (PBT) was calculated at a 3% increase coupled to some cost savings as well involving a proposal to reduce the headcount of field-based sales staff given the rapid rise in other suppliers moving to online sales.

This didn't sound like the shift that was expected at the beginning of a new appointment as Sales Director, especially since Lindsay had heard from Mike (they both joined JENZZO at the same time), Amy and Sylvia about some interesting developments from an internal group working on a special project called Plan B. Lindsay knew they were overseeing the launch of a new product and a major change to their traditional sales process having been given access to the plans.

Lindsay had also been doing some thinking in the build-up to the budget meeting and had made some preparations having come across something called the Rubicon Performance Leap process which sounded extremely useful (see Figure 11).

Lindsay had also felt for a long time that the more career progress made up the company's hierarchy, the more pressure was applied to think differently compared to the natural inclination of the past. It was noticeable that the people who had most influence or power in senior management roles tended to apply more logic and critical thinking and numerical tendencies. Whereas Lindsay had always been good at reading emotions, using imagination and being creative.

There was something in this numerical approach that reminded Lindsay of 'Reductionism'[1] which is the practice of analysing a complex phenomenon in terms of its simple constituents, especially when this is said to provide a sufficient explanation of the whole. In the past, a thought had often struck Lindsay about components being considered together as a whole which could have qualities that delivered more than the total of all the individual parts. This holistic view had become somewhat of a fascination and further research had thrown up a theory to describe the phenomenon – 'Gestalt' Theory[2]. It was something that would occasionally guide Lindsay in serious discussions.

Also, a friend had pointed out, whether myth or not, that some people have a left brain tendency and some a right brain tendency[3]. The friend thought Lindsay fell into the right brain camp. The friend went on to say that there is no disadvantage in either camp and that Lindsay could do well with innovation and inspiration, rather than say, engineering or accountancy. Lindsay felt reassured by the feedback.

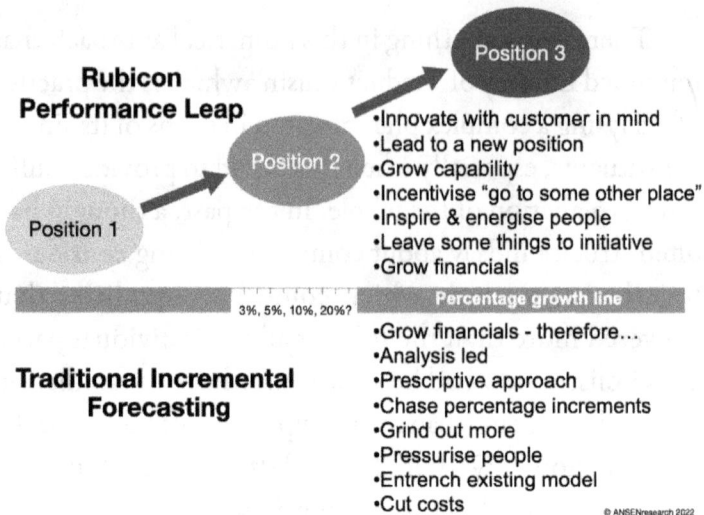

Figure 11: Rubicon Performance Leap

If you continue to do the same as everyone else, you will get the same results

Lindsay had also been watching a few sales training videos on YouTube. One was a TEDxMaastricht[4] presentation that seemed incredibly useful. It involved Paul Rulkens and was entitled "*Why the Majority is Always Wrong*". Rulkens begins by telling the audience about an examination that Einstein set in 1942 for his senior physics students. Afterwards, his assistant asked Einstein, "Isn't that the same exam you gave to exactly the same class one year ago?".

"Yes, exactly the same..." replied Einstein.

"Why would you do that?" asked the assistant.

"Because the answers have changed!" responded Einstein.

The same is true today, what has got you here will not get you to where you need to be.

The general thrust of the video was if you continue to do the same as everyone else, you will likely get the same results. This rang a bell with Lindsay and confirmed the idea of following the Rubicon Performance Leap and not the orthodox path of grinding out another 3% by asking people to work harder, do more sales calls and work more hours.

> *What has got you here will not get you to where you need to be*

When the annual budget day arrived, Lindsay placed faith in 'right brain' thinking, Performance Leaps, Gestalt Theory and Plan B, and said that the sales team would commit to a 20% increase in revenue but with the proviso for some extra resources in a few places and no reduction in the sales and service headcount. The room was silent for a few seconds and then Charlie and Nico said in unison "that's a brave shout!". Charlie went on to say, "you do realise we will judge you and the Field Teams to perform to that?" and Lindsay nodded, left the room and gulped nervously at the prospect.

Lindsay now knew that Plan B and the new telematics and CRM systems would be crucial to hitting the target. Lindsay also guessed correctly that the CEO would also grant some tolerance if things didn't go to plan in the first year, provided progress was seen to be made; after all, the visit from the Chairperson had not been lost on the CEO. Aiming for perfection would not be allowed to spoil the good! Lindsay had crossed the Rubicon into the land of Advanced Services. There would need to be others.

Summary & Resources

This short chapter has pinpointed a fresh approach to creating bolder visions and ways of achieving better but less financially structured goals. The idea of moving away from 'grinding' better results from the same systems and resources together with throwing in some cost cuts can work for a while, but the bolder steps to achieve breakthrough performance requires a more inspired but somewhat looser assembly of components where initiative and inspiration towards a common goal can create bigger strides. Following company orthodoxy can be a safe bet but will not necessarily lead to exceptional or exponential results.

[1] *Reductionism*
https://sk.sagepub.com/ency/edvol/
sage-encyclopedia-of-business-ethics-and-society-2e/chpt/reductionism

[2] *Gestalt Theory*
https://dictionary.cambridge.org/dictionary/english/gestalt

[3] *Right brain/left brain, right?*
https://www.health.harvard.edu/blog/
right-brainleft-brain-right-2017082512222

[4] *TedX - Why the Majority is Always Wrong*, Paul Rulkens
https://tedtalkswalks.medium.com/
why-the-majority-is-always-wrong-paul-rulkens-30b2c425570d

CHAPTER 8

Know Your Customer (KYC)

Many years ago a group of colleagues and I met with Richard Mayer[1], then a Senior Lecturer in Marketing at Derby University, UK. We were in search of ideas to boost our marketing capability, using our extensive database.

His first ask and our main take-away was "show me your recency, frequency, profitability table". We needed an explanation and after discussing the matter, we returned to our office to create such a table.

Recency Frequency Profitability Table

I'll call it the Rubicon Recency/Frequency/Profitability table or RFP for short (see mock-up in Figure 12). Each category is awarded a token score based on factors to suit the business. In this case the mock-up shows a sample of only five Customers of JENZZO Group. Each RFP column is selectable and will place in descending or ascending order the score across the whole Customer portfolio or selected regions or individuals. If using colour, the hotter the score the more red bias. Cold scores move to blue.

Most of the magic happens when Recency is selected in ascending order and the table immediately shows which Customers have been neglected. They haven't bought equipment for a while and questions need to be asked if they were previously frequent buyers, especially if they were also profitable to deal with.

Rubicon Recency/Frequency/Profitability Table

Customer	Recency	Frequency	Profit	Score
Phillips Port Handlers	5	5	5	15
Johnson Rail	4	3	3	10
Green Waste	3	4	1	8
Billy's Waste	2	2	5	9
Midtown Council	1	4	4	9

Key	Latest Transaction in Months	Frequency i.e. Number of Units	Profit in latest 5 Years	
5	≤ 6 Months	> 5	≥ €50,000	
4	> 6 but ≤12	5	<€50,000 but ≥€40,000	
3	>12 but ≤24	4	<€40,000 but ≥€20,000	
2	>24 but ≤36	<4 but >1	<€20,000 but ≥€10,000	
1	>36	≤1	<€10,000	

Figure 12: Recency, Frequency, Profitability Table

There are plenty of things in play, even with a sample of only five Customers, such as:

- Phillips Port Handlers with all high/red scores can perhaps be left alone a little.
- Billy's Waste are neither recent nor frequent, and yet have been profitable in the past. The question 'why?' shines out.

- Green Waste have been fairly frequent but not recent and were not profitable. Was this an attribute of the transaction value or were margins too thin on the dealings?

The RFP analysis can go on. The essential outcome is that the JENZZO Group Sales & Marketing Team need to adopt this and look at those Customers who were frequent and profitable but who have not been recent by searching for the cooler scores/colours in those categories <u>and then follow them up!</u>

Customer Segregation

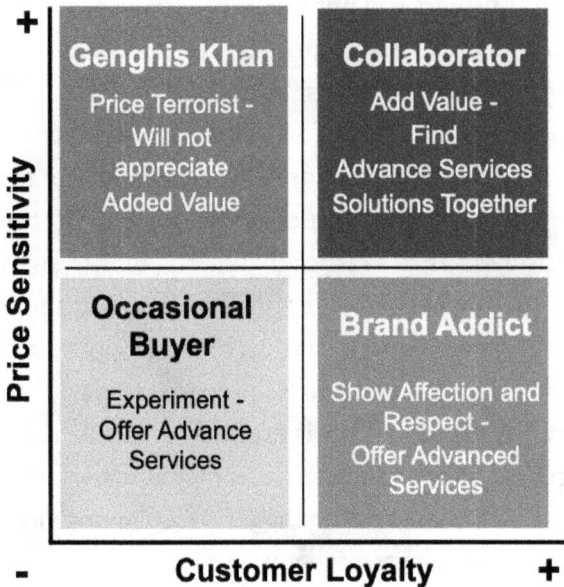

Figure 13: Rubicon Price & Loyalty Matrix (PLM)

There are many ways to segregate Customers but the Rubicon Price & Loyalty Matrix (PLM) (see Figure 13) will help the Plan B Team to select those Customers with the best characteristics to take up Advanced Services.

- **'Genghis Khan'** - These Customers will only deal with JENZZO when the price is screwed to the floor. They will do this with all suppliers. It may still be worthwhile to deal with them perhaps because of the overall size of business transactions, but JENZZO must accept that dealings are likely to be strictly on a minimum margin basis. Even providing hospitality and other incentives will not create any goodwill or loyalty.
- **'Collaborator'** - This Customer is likely to be a larger business too but its leadership is inclined to listen and explore options with JENZZO. Pricing will still be tight due to the high level of sophistication of the Customer. They are likely to take proper advantage of service contracts and keep their own personnel focused on solving their Customers' issues rather than fixing breakdowns or conducting maintenance on JENZZO's equipment. That is left to an expectation of fast response service back-up for which they are prepared to pay.
- **'Brand Addict'** - This is probably a 'salt-of-the-earth', less sophisticated Customer and an outfit that enjoys the kudos of buying JENZZO equipment. They should be treated with affection and respect and will respond to gestures of goodwill made to them. They would probably enjoy the attention if

100

JENZZO were to explore some Advanced Services together with them.

- **'Occasional Buyer'** - This Customer has probably got a single use for the JENZZO product and may not return to the market for some time. JENZZO should keep in touch to 'catch them in the act of buying'. This Customer will probably not see JENZZO as a favoured supplier to a great degree unless long-term experience indicates otherwise. Pitching Advanced Services could be useful in some buying situations.

Using the RFP and PLM will not necessarily yield immediate results for their own product in the new airport sector because they hold no data yet, but it may help the Plan B Team to influence other internal stakeholders by trading the intellectual model and processes for advocacy in what they are working on. The internal innovation will have value and cause changes within their own IT, Marketing and Sales Teams. The same model could be used for analysing the Service Team's records for parts, warranty and other metrics.

The RFP table can become the platform to engage with Customers during sales canvassing sessions that should take place on a regular basis with interaction recorded on the CRM system against each call to assess the number of calls made, decision makers reached, appointments scheduled and proposals received for new business. The activity should become part of the individual performance management regime – more on that later.

The RFP will also highlight over-reliance on certain accounts and could overlap with debtor control processes.

Warranty Claims

Handling of equipment warranty claims could form a book in itself, but the areas I'm interested in are fourfold.

Known hot-spots of equipment failures as a result of inherent manufacturing defect are, no doubt, actioned straight away, but if we place this to one side we're probably left with 'sympathetic' or other unworthy warranty claims.

There are a few pernicious matters of concern regarding Warranty operations when linked to KYC and service contracts such as:

- Favouritism shown to a Customer overriding commercial common sense – a costly failing.
- Poor quality service delivery causing early failure of parts or predictable failures.
- Machinery abuse which is tolerated because the Customer has placed forward orders and confronting that abuse could jeopardise those future orders.
- Mismatch of product design life or equipment application, especially where the Customer (or salesperson) has selected a lower cost/specification product to undertake an arduous task to minimise the contract price point.

Revenue is compromised in each case but there is a further impact which is regularly either purposely ignored or not considered through ignorance. JENZZO's leasing partner, C Leasing, may be the actual owner of the equipment and have the contractual or moral right to know what is taking place with the equipment it owns, especially when on-going poor service standards or abuse of equipment is identified. If C Leasing had to foreclose on a lease because of non-payment of rentals by the Customer, the equipment will be returned in a poor state and re-marketing will be compromised, exacerbating the loss the leasing company will make, and shaking its belief in the quality of the equipment and/or service operations being conducted by JENZZO and any partners. Off-loading distressed products can seriously harm market value perceptions.

> *Poor service provision by JENZZO*
> *could also prompt suspension of*
> *leasing rentals by the Customer*

Poor service provision by JENZZO and its agents could also prompt suspension of leasing rentals by the Customer, again harming the interests of C Leasing. Sylvia will have some colourful stories to tell on both of these issues, hopefully not involving many JENZZO transactions.

I've known product engineers proudly announce that product X now has an improved design life of 10,000 hours. Problems arise when the sales and marketing side of the business are promoting five-year (or longer) contracts bearing 2,000 hours per annum in fairly arduous applications. Two immediate factors are evident – residual values are difficult to set – who will want to buy such a product bearing 10,000 hours or more at the end of five years? Also, the service side of the business may not favour long-term repair and maintenance cover given that the risk of product structures or major component failure increases with time. The Customer and leasing company could find themselves facing increasing reluctance to receive contracted breakdown cover towards the end of the contract if a major failure occurs.

In-depth knowledge of the Customer, their behaviours, equipment application and service oversight can mitigate some of the dilemmas mentioned above.

Helpful Business Models

There are some simple models that can help to gain a deeper understanding of a Customer or a potential Customer and these are worth exploring in the next few pages. They can help with Sales Transformation and Selling in a Service-Based way by giving an edge to help the Customer make a favourable decision plus mitigate contractual risks.

Three-Legged Stool Model

I like this model because it's simple but powerful. Sylvia from C Leasing has probably been coached to use this when trying to get a proper picture of a Customer prior to considering a credit proposal for leasing contracts. The three legs consist of:

- **Know the Customer**
- **Know the Customer's business**
- **Know how the business is funded**

Know the Customer - This about identifying and getting the background and measure of the people operating and controlling the business.

Know the Customer's Business - This about understanding how the business is structured and what it actually does plus where it stands in the market it operates and does it possess a concentration risk of trading too much with one entity.

Know How the Business is Funded - Looks at the main financial stakeholders. They might be family members, public or private shareholders, stockholders, private equity businesses, directors' loans, banks eg loans and overdrafts, leasing and asset finance firms, creditors, Tax Authorities, Local Authorities etc. What margins of liquidity does the business operate with? In other words, are they operating on the edge of their agreed terms with any entity to whom they owe money? What has been their track record and what predictions can be made about the medium-term survival or viability?

All three categories can lead to uncovering useful ways to interpret the potential behaviour and the context of the Customer's position when considering a new business proposition. The information can often be put together even before an initial approach to do business.

Six Cs Formula Table

Character	Collateral
Capacity	Condition
Capital	Completion

This analysis model goes further than the Three Legged Stool and provides a memorable alliteration to help with the assessment.

Character - What is the standing of the prospect within the business sector. How do they behave during negotiations? Are they honest? Can we trust them? How assertive are they and how do they treat us? What are their known dealings with suppliers or other entities? This section is trying to determine the overall reputation and reliability of who we might be dealing with.

Capacity - Does the Customer have the capacity to take on what we may be about to propose? What are the skills and resources available to make superior use of what we are putting together in our business proposal?

Capital - As the heading suggests, what financial resources are available to the Customer to make this project a success throughout the duration of its expected useful working life?

Collateral - In a lending sense, C Leasing would want to assess what security is available in a foreclosure situation. If our imaginary proposal is about JENZZO Group granting a contract for the long-term supply of expensive equipment, ie JENZZO funds it, how can we ensure we don't make a loss if the project or the Customer fails financially? If we supply parts or consumables, do we have terms of supply on the invoice or elsewhere that include retaining title to the equipment and stores and right of access to retrieve such goods?

Condition - What conditions are prevailing or predicted that could impact on the marketplace in which the Customer trades? Today, there are new risks emerging especially in respect of trading terms or meeting Net Zero obligations. Could equipment obsolescence create difficulties in the medium term? Are there emerging technologies or power sources that could threaten the viability of the proposed project? What can be done to mitigate such threats? What is the level of emerging threat from low-cost producers?

Completion - What is the history of the Customer completing projects or contracts in the past? Have they ever shown an element of difficulty in completing deadlines or set production targets? How quickly or slowly have they reacted to proposals in the past and could tardiness lead to unexpected costs on one or both sides?

Rubicon Forcefield Analysis

The following graphic (see Figure 14) illustrates a tool that is useful in decision making. There will be good reasons to undertake an advanced services contract but there could also be risks substantial enough not to take it ahead.

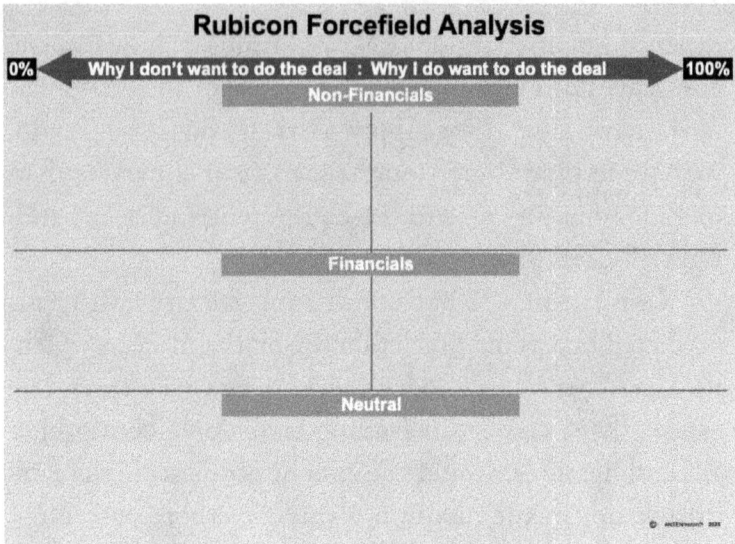

Figure 14: Rubicon Forcefield Analysis

The tool is divided into three horizontal layers. The top level relates to non-financial issues that have been gathered which either give confidence to go ahead or not.

The right side is concerned with listing all the reasons that justify going ahead. The left side is concerned with listing reasons to cease progress. The lists can be as long as necessary.

Any non-financial issues listed that could weigh on a decision, either positively or negatively can be assessed; likewise, financials can be noted. Each line of comment can be scored down to 0% = zero appetite, or up to 100% = absolute appetite. Of course, some scores will relate to major factors, others relatively less consequential but could mount up in aggregate. The final position can be subjectively assessed to form a preliminary opinion based on whether the positive comments appear to outweigh the negatives or not.

The 'Neutral' section at the foot of the analysis is intended to list additional background information, issues or questions that require further clarification. The analysis should be sketched out before a meeting but is not intended for use in front of the Customer. Clear answers to any questions allow further input into the top two layers.

This simple tool is intended to provide stimulus for progress by creating qualitative information to enable a well-structured discussion with the Customer to take place. This will ultimately provide justification for us to move ahead with a deal or not and in the meanwhile create confidence for the Customer by showing that we are a professional, well-informed organisation worthy of placing business with.

Summary & Resources
The simple 'Know Your Customer' tools described in this chapter cover some of the fundamentals to allow a better understanding of who the Customer is, the background conditions that face them and also some useful purchasing behavioural information.

It is the beginning of creating disciplines that will be needed to assess opportunities and risks while forging the approach involved in new advance services. This will act as an aid to discovering the outcomes that Customers could need in the future. Some of those needs may not even be on the Customers' radar because no-one has consulted closely enough to identify what can be delivered beyond the traditional model of equipment sales and related after-market services to maintain up-time of that equipment used within the Customers' operations.

The new world order involving tariff shockwaves and Net Zero pressures will call for new approaches to stimulate deeper collaborative relationships and understandings for mutual benefit. A new set of perceived drivers will offer up a range of opportunities for those manufacturers and Customers who are adroit and agile enough to exploit the new circumstances.

[1] *Richard Mayer, Senior Lecturer in Marketing at Derby University*
https://www.linkedin.com/in/richard-mayer2020/

CHAPTER 9

Building a Rubicon Cult

A senior banking colleague attended an annual internal Company conference that I hosted a few years ago in South Wales. He enjoyed the event with its usual review of year-end performances and forward outlooks plus various speakers and a coaching session.

Some of the Company Team volunteered to stay behind at our office and respond to Customer phone calls etc. We set up a new-fangled (at the time) video link so that the HQ Team could join in.

The various sessions went well and plenty of motivation was on show. At one point my colleague turned to me and said, "Paul, you haven't got a Company Team here, you've got a cult!". That was about the best thing he could have said to me about what had been built by so many talented people stretching back to the Company's formation in 1970.

Someone else said to me once, "I don't know how so many people can work at the same place for so long".

I smiled and thought about the fact that the business had not stayed the same. It had writhed with change for its whole existence, from its early pioneering days to a more mature business. In fact, the pace of change continuously accelerated even through the financial crash of 2008-2014. Ambition presented new challenges and opened up new opportunities as a result. Change was a friend.

An important aspect of moving on is that sometimes you have to pay respects to the way things used to be done – give it an honourable funeral while accepting the incoming new ways. A funeral also demonstrates that we're not going back, the Rubicon has been crossed.

Building a Cult – In It Together

As a result of my banking colleague's comments, I thought about the old adage that goes something like 'Are you here to lay bricks, build a wall or build a cathedral?'. Thereafter, I thought about an additional task '... or build a cult?' – I liked the idea of us building our cult together!

During my career I was coached either purposefully or subconsciously by so many good, conscientious people to focus on what we were doing for the Customer. What the Customer was trying to achieve within the sectors they operated. For instance, in construction it was about the built environment. Helping construction businesses to invest in the right equipment to achieve the end result. House building was a favourite of mine because of the chronic housing shortage in the UK. We were committed to contributing to relieve the hardship confronting people who couldn't get onto the housing ladder because of housing scarcity and the attendant high cost of finding a home. Much time was spent with organisations such as the UK's Federation of Master Builders or the National Federation of Builders to see how we could jointly help. This kind of deep-seated activity fed through to the whole Company so that everyone could share in that mission rather than simply doing a 9-to-5 job.

A surprise email from a Government Official one Saturday afternoon in early 2014 was an invitation to go to 10 Downing Street to work with Officials to find improved ways to get investment funds into the housing sector. This was bolstered by breakfast meetings with Members of Parliament at the Palace of Westminster to stress the difficulties with the UK's planning regulations and other impediments hampering a return to large scale house building volumes.

We had been noticed because at one stage of the Financial Crisis we were providing around one third of the leasing facilities used by UK Local Authorities to fund their purchases of construction equipment, but it went beyond this to include trucks, refuse trucks, vans, cars, even fire engines, school kitchen equipment and several crematorium furnaces! We attended one of the first Road Shows of the new British Business Bank that was set up to aid the return to liquidity into the economy following the Financial Crash of 2008.

We mobilised Emotional Intelligence

The Covid pandemic saw us as one of the lead institutions in co-ordinating the response of asset finance lenders as leasing payment breaks were introduced across the nation followed by the introduction of emergency loans to help UK businesses survive.

Some Customers were at the end of their tether. Over the course of a fortnight after the lockdown was announced, thousands of our Customers received a personal phone call from our staff with an to offer help. There were people in tears in reaction to such empathy, compassion and immediacy. We mobilised Emotional Intelligence.

Similar initiatives were previously put into place at pace to help farming Customers during the 2001 UK Foot & Mouth disease outbreak on cattle and sheep farms.

The Company Team were either directly involved or continuously briefed about the steps and initiatives that were put in place. It would be extremely difficult to replicate this emotional impact with AI. Everyone was doing their bit and recognised that the business was focused on making a difference. The impact was giving people a sense of purpose at work and reinforcing that strong self-esteem mentioned earlier.

Having Fun

Over my 50-year career one of the personal and prime objectives was to have fun coupled with purpose. This was achieved in so many ways and with so many people. It always seemed to me that part of the joy of working was being with other people and achieving tasks for wider benefit. I began to lead small teams in 1984 aged 27. OK, empires can rise and fall in five years – I'm not talking about helping in those days to create an overnight £1bn unicorn, yet.

Up to that point, as a young lad, I had been regularly entrusted with fairly important company information. This impressed me and was a sign that I was 'in with the in-crowd'. It also meant that I felt enabled and keen to provide constructive feedback on fairly important company issues. Similar things happened when I passed on company information to colleagues for whom I was responsible.

The idea of having fun and plenty of laughter along the way was infectious and added a stimulus that tempted more discretionary effort out of almost everyone.

Resilience – Personal Reflections

My family life has been the bedrock of my existence but very often the work/life balance seemed to have a very blurred dividing line that suited me down to the ground. Despite being a salaried young married man with young children, I still found the motivation to be in the office at 7.00am twice a week and hardly ever left before 6.30pm, sometimes 9.30pm. Saturday mornings were when our children learned how to use photocopiers and Microsoft 'Paint' at the office. Nights away from home or jumping on a plane at short notice were regular events. For me, mowing the lawn, taking a bath or going to bed were times to think. Bolstered by the love and support from my family, I rarely had low moments at work and learned a lot from them anyway.

Managing a Team

I really appreciate team harmony. Recruiting the right people and managing a team's composition is a vital task. Recruitment is an art in itself and fills many bookshelves so it's not my intention to delve deeply into the topic here except to say that during recruitment meetings I always looked for 'brightness' coupled with some appropriate experience or academic qualifications. After a warm welcome, an initial couple of questions usually set the format for the rest of an interview such as, "Thank you for your interest, what do you already know about our business?" or "What has moved you to want to work here?". A blank stare would not be a good start.

There are occasions where an individual's fit becomes untenable and action has to be taken, and be seen to be taken, to rebalance things where something is going wrong. It's tough work to be face to face with someone who has reached a point of destabilising the harmony beyond the point of no return. They have to go and a humane exit has to be arranged. There should be no feeling of shame or guilt about the process.

Team harmony takes hard work and constant vigilance to foster it. A crucial lesson to be learnt is that corporate life is sometimes not a bed of roses, especially when you're leading change projects.

Change management does sometimes involve bumping into significant resistance, both internally and externally, and some of that resistance can be doggedly designed and orchestrated to undermine the desired progress. Hopefully you will give and receive automatic and appropriate support to and from the top. However, even then, it may not be full of peace and tranquillity, and the need for results can, unfortunately, outweigh handing flowers to each other. These occasions are very much a minority but if you stand for something you must recognise, and be recognised for, the need to stand your ground.

Don't let the bastards get you down!

On the personal side, if I got into occasional political squabbles that can naturally break out, and if these arrived at an impasse, I'd talk them through with my wife and receive a confidence boost. In extremis, I'd clutch a small sterling silver pendant she had given me that hung off my briefcase engraved with the words 'Don't let the bastards get you down!'. I could still have a chuckle at most of the difficult times even though it wasn't pretty.

It's well worth remembering that there will be neutral by-standers and if you stay true to the objective and demonstrate rightful commitment for a greater cause, you will garner respect eventually.

A couple of time-served general business anecdotes might serve well here. Firstly, while competing for market share against Kodak, the Japanese firm, Fuji Film, had a public Mission Statement "Giving our world more smiles", denoting their commitment to innovate in the area of imagery, but the motivational message to internal staff was somewhat different, brief and brutal "Kill Kodak!".

A further acerbic example comes from Ray Kroc who,

some would say, was notorious in his early years as CEO of McDonald's. He came up with the quote "If my competitor were drowning, I'd stick a hose in his mouth and turn on the water". He was rightly criticised for the phrase but while most of us would not embrace this brutal viewpoint, we have to remember that an opponent in business, or within a simple clash of ideas, may well do so. Be Prepared.

Of course, there is much more that is involved in shaping and dealing with culture within an organisation, but I hope the above anecdotes serve as useful and entertaining examples.

Cult Achievements

By way of demonstration of what a properly motivated team can do, some public data from UK Companies House shows the following picture at JCB Finance Ltd. I was appointed as Sales Director in 2004 and CEO in 2011. The Pre-Tax Profit in the five years prior to 2004 averaged £3.5m. During my eight-year tenure as Sales Director the average rose to £6.7m and as CEO for the next 11 years rose to an annual average of £24.1m[1]. This wasn't my achievement, it was evidence of what an energised and resource-enabled team could do, building on past achievements. Headcount grew in that time from around 70 to 100 people with most growth in Sales, IT and Risk Management.

In 2019 the team at JCB Finance Ltd broke through the £1bn Customer lending level for the first time and on the back of that, received a prestigious award from the International Asset Finance Network as European

Captive Finance Lessor of 2019. Shortly after this, the team transitioned seamlessly to home working on the first day of the Covid-19 Lockdown and became influential in the asset finance sector's navigation of regulatory and legal compliance with the introduction of immediate lease rental pauses and emergency funding assistance to UK businesses during the pandemic.

At the end of my 11-year tenure as CEO, the business had paid out £200m in dividends (per public records) to the shareholders. Not a bad result for a team of around one hundred people head-quartered in leafy rural Staffordshire.

Joy was to be had in working with an amazing team of people who constantly, even obsessively, went out of their way to ensure Customers were looked after, year after year, which was borne out by the published Net Promoter Score[2] regularly standing at over **80**.

To give that NPS Score some context:
- NatWest[3] for Commercial Banking in England & Wales for Q4 2024 -7 and Commercial Mid-Banking was **5**.
- Netflix[4] December 2024-February 2025 was **43**.
- Apple[5] 2024 **61**.

Above all, amidst this professionalism, we were still having fun and, I hope, finding a great sense of achievement together before I retired in July 2022.

Permit me to further mention on the personal side that after 40 years plus of being an Associate of the Chartered Institute of Bankers I received an Honorary Fellowship of the London Institute of Banking and Finance and became a Fellow of the Chartered Management Institute through my studies from 2003-2007 and the winning of their annual Sir Henry Fildes national award in 2007.

In 2022 I was appointed as a Visiting Professor at the College of Business and Social Sciences at Aston University, Birmingham, UK. My retirement from full-time employment meant also retiring as a Board Director of the London-based Finance & Leasing Association and Chair of their Asset Finance Division. I was proud to receive the 2022 Lifetime Achievement Award from the Asset Finance Connect organisation.

I hope these very personal reflections provide fertile ground for ideas about sparking and managing change to support your project.

There are some building blocks that I would recommend to increase performance and aid the successful Servitization transition:

- Adopting a performance leap approach.
- Create a Rubicon frontier and followers willing to cross it.
- 'Change the People or Change the People' involving the assessment of skills and willingness to embrace change.
- Improve Performance Metrics Dashboards.
- Weekly Teleconferences and diary checks with key people.
- Variable Pay schemes should be aligned to Stretch Targets.
- Tight Performance Management and oversight.
- Introduce a new business Pipeline with a RAG

'Promise' System providing lead indicators.
- Stay ahead on Customer Contract delivery methods including online.
- Establish a Direct Sales Team.
- Introduce dedicated National/Key Accounts coverage.
- Align Dealer incentives plus intensify Dealer coaching.
- Differentiate Advanced Services Contracts and products.
- Canvass using a Recency/Frequency/Profitability Matrix.
- Invest significant money in sophisticated Point of Sale IT/Apps linked seamlessly to a range of back-office functions.
- Use AI within a Contract Uptake Probability Score engine.
- Marketing has to be relentless with carefully choreographed messages.
- Asset Management (dealing with used equipment, setting residual values etc) has to be first rate and cultivate a trading profile.
- Make sure everyone shares deep Customer empathy.
- Sponsor fresh academic qualifications.
- Be prepared to 'over-communicate' with your Board and other stakeholders.

Most of these blocks can probably be accomplished 'in-house' although reaching out for external expert assistance when required is extremely valuable and cuts down delivery timescales.

Now back to JENZZO and addressing the business transformation that was knocking on their door. Inspiring their people and stakeholders to take a new *performance leap* was not going to be an easy task. Staff who had control over naughty little spreadsheets that were essential to key system work-arounds would start to feel the loss of their personal custodianship from which they had derived satisfaction for years. So many times in the past, colleagues had found themselves saying that Jose or Aisha were on holiday and the Customer's query would have to wait until their return in a few days as they were the only people who knew the answer! In that regard, I was once cautioned to remember that "the graveyards are full of indispensable people!".

JENZZO would eventually have to have an honourable funeral for their business model of simply selling goods, selling spare parts and signing up some service contracts and cross the Rubicon to become a committed servitization centre of excellence.

Summary & Resources

In this chapter we've seen the difference that having a fully engaged and inspired team can achieve. Change is sometimes feared or perhaps reluctantly embraced, but if it becomes a fundamental and continuous part of the culture of a business, some really great things can happen.

If our fictional JENZZO company is going to pivot to advanced services, Mike, the Plan B Project Group and their Executive Team have some serious work to do to take their whole organisation with them on this journey.

In the next chapters we're going to see how they embrace transforming their sales approach to allow them to move away from selling capital equipment mostly based on price, and align themselves to justifying cost in a different way by involving a more formal relationship with their Sales-Aid Finance partner. They will ultimately need to design a flexible platform together that delivers options to seamlessly handle bundled services and consumables.

[1] JCB Finance Ltd 2019 results were boosted by hive up from subsidiary.

[2] *Net Promoter Score Explanation.*
https://contentsquare.com/guides/net-promoter-score/

[3] *NatWest NPS Scores*
https://www.natwestgroup.com/sustainability/
society/customer-advocacy.html

[4] *Netflix NPS Scores*
https://altindex.com/ticker/nflx/nps

[5] *Apple NPS Scores*
https://www.questionpro.com/blog/
apple-nps/#Apples_Net_Promoter_Score

CHAPTER 10

How to Transform Sales

Here's a simple case study of a sales call to emphasise a couple of important points. Let's place ourselves in Jenzzo's sales office overhearing a new phone enquiry being handled by young Jake within the Sales Team.

Sales Enquiry - Scenario 1

"Hi," says Françoise at the start of an incoming enquiry – she's in charge of operations for a fairly substantial Customer. "I'm interested in one of your big XP31 machines."

"That's great" says Jake, "I'm so glad you're impressed, Françoise, they're a super unit, we sell a lot."

"How much is it?" says Françoise.

Jake now feels under the usual and immediate pressure of a potentially early incoming price objection (it happens every time!). "Err, well the XP31 comes equipped with a lot more capabilities than the competition and has some really good features."

We're now in real trouble because:

- Even the use of the word 'competition' cranks up Jake's own psychological discomfort; and
- Françoise is now alerted about alternatives; and
- It sounds as if the XP31 is going to be unjustifiably expensive because Jake daren't give a price with any confidence!

There is silence. Eventually Jake spurts out, "Err, it's around €128,000."

Now there's something strange about being a human. Any person who receives a price like this seems to have their DNA primed to immediately pout their lips, ingest a sharp intake of breath followed by an exhale, muttering, as Françoise did, "Wow, that's too much!". They regularly go on to say, "Send me a quote and I'll think about it", and terminate the enquiry, which she did.

It's as predictable as night follows day, isn't it?

Jake says, "Thanks, I'll get right on to it", and then wastes the time of two other people in preparing a quote for the XP31 to confirm the unacceptable news he's just given. Jake comforts himself that this was just a general query and feels that the Customer might be back. Although Jake doesn't like the idea of being a price crumbler, the idea of heavily discounting the price began to perch on Jake's shoulders. He then goes to make a coffee for the other two colleagues.

Sales-Aid Finance

Moving on from Jake's situation, we can consider how Sales-Aid Finance could aid the sale. This is a method of running a funding option alongside selling a product or service. We all see it in everyday life, whether it's a credit card at a shop, online 'Buy Now Pay Later schemes' (BNPL), insurance premium credit, fuel accounts and moving up the value chain to the car finance we covered earlier. The idea is that the Customer doesn't pay for the goods or service immediately, allowing the purchase to be immediate, convenient, almost painless in that moment for the Customer, but also carrying a perspective of affordability whilst being a conclusive, rewarding and persuasive instrument for the seller.

For many capital purchases or investments, and most likely in the business world, there is a financial organisation in the middle providing some money at a set rate of return for the short-, medium- or long-term to enable the transaction to go ahead. Repayments will either be made in full at a certain time (a 'bullet' payment) or multiple repayments will be made over a certain length of time at predetermined dates and levels.

The objective is for the whole operation to be as slick as possible so that the Customer and seller find it easy and swift to use to conclude their piece of business together. When it works right, it can be a very useful sales tool to help the Customer to buy and help the seller to sell. Experience shows that the salespeople who use sales-aid finance sell more kit and earn more money as a result.

Let us now assume that Jake has access to a sales-aid solution and see if he can handle the same enquiry from Françoise any better.

Sales Enquiry – Scenario 2

"Hi," says Françoise, the Customer, "I'm interested in one of your big XP31 machines."

"That's great," says Jake, "I'm so glad you're impressed, they're a super unit, and generate good returns."

"How much is it?" says Françoise.

Jake fires back: "Give me a second, Françoise, let me just have a look at my [Sales-Aid Finance] system, yeah, it's going to be around €115 a day if you're working five days a week."

"But I work six days a week!" snaps Françoise.

"Then it's going to be even less per day!" says Jake with a smile down the phone.

"Hmmm, tell me how you do that," says Françoise without the immediate and usual DNA-inspired sharp intake of breath and auto-pout. The price objection will indeed come, but an important idea has been planted in her ear before it arrives.

Jake has quickly used a simple lease calculator that Sylvia supplied to him to work out repayments based on a 60-month term with a low € sum payable at the start and a large, deferred sum (Residual Value) payable at the end that will be recovered when the machine is returned to C Leasing to be re-marketed through Jenzzo's network. This picture is still using fairly rudimentary skills but is using 'Sales-Aid Finance' to aid the negotiation, taking immediate pressure off the cash price and beginning the investment justification process with a degree of negotiating control now resting with Jake. After all, there is a huge difference between the first 'number' quoted in this call of 115 compared to 128,000 in scenario one.

It is the beginning of a consultative sale that could help the Customer buy and it won't call for an immediate, worthless but expensive looking quote that gets put in a drawer.

The Customer will still get to know the cash price when Jake feels it's time – after all, he's been asked to explain something else first. Obviously if the Customer doesn't want to take up a lease the price will continue to suffer the usual price objection, but what has happened is that Jake has positioned a figure in the Customer's head that will now tie in with her own perceptions and interpretation about affordability and investment justification for an XP31 machine within her overall production process. That €115 a day (or even less for six-day working!) will not go away easily – even if she somehow ultimately pays cash. Jake has given her an immediate and good context upon which to consider the deal further.

With XaaS, we can no longer sell using a cash price with the Customer

Does this approach work every time? – No, definitely not, some Customers would think Jake was from the Planet Zog. Will it cause a deal to close there and then? – No, definitely not, but when Jake thinks it could be useful, he'll employ it – that is, when it feels right!

However, if we are to transition to 'Product-as-a-Service' (PaaS), Capacity-as-a-Service (CaaS) or *AnythingElse*-as-a-Service (XaaS), how will Jake cope if he tries Scenario 1 ever again? With XaaS, we can no longer sell using a cash price with the Customer – because there simply isn't one! We'll revisit this in the next chapter. It's beginning to feel that the old days and the old ways will have to receive that honourable funeral.

Lag & Lead – The Story of Cheetah Droppings

Let us imagine that our internal processes provide us with a huge quantity of data, especially numerical, about what the Customer has done with us in the past. We can examine the data in microscopic detail and decide that this is the backbone of our sales and marketing outlook. Of course, most of this is 'lag' information. Some of it, eg the 'Rubicon RFP', can be an excellent predictor of which Customers should be contacted, but lag information is a bit like cheetah droppings. While on safari, on the trail of our cheetah, we can obtain a lot of information about the latest meal that the fastest land mammal consumed and when it happened. Unfortunately, we cannot predict where or when or what the cheetah will stalk, chase and maybe catch next to feed herself and her cubs. This lead information can be very elusive but because it is difficult, it doesn't mean that it should be ignored.

I remember an old phrase "we should not simply value what we measure, we should measure what we value".

Another phrase comes to mind too – "Are we continually weighing the pig instead of fattening it?" – maybe the cheetah would be interested?

New Business Pipeline

The type of lead indicators that I favour are either outcomes of Customer direct interactions or indirect and based on predictive behaviours. Logging of both types allows for a pipeline of potential new business flows. A system that allows the Sales Team or AI to give scores to that potential increases the usefulness. A Red/Amber/Green (RAG) score increases the reliability. See following table (Figure 15).

Status	Classification
Green	90%+ likelihood of a new transaction within one month
Amber	60%+ likelihood of a new transaction within one month
Red	Record of speculative work taking place to generate a lead but without new business potential within one month.

Figure 15: Pipeline Promises – Definitions

Each Salesperson or AI Agent has their own pipeline with the object being to move Red to Amber and Amber to Green and then close a deal. The classifications are firm promises made personally to the Sales Director and a log is used to keep the system honest by ensuring that individual green records are not 'played' by being continuously rolled over to the next period. The idea is that Sales Management adds a little pressure or support to aid proposed deals to move from one classification up to the next. Sales Management also sees the likely activity levels being undertaken by each introducer and can take corrective action via their internal performance management process or reshaping algorithms.

'N' Months to Run Data

If JENZZO are working closely with C Leasing they may be able to unlock an extremely useful lead data set that is as old as the hills in the leasing world. This is generated from the portfolio of Customer lease records that can be analysed to show which transactions are coming to the end of their contracted term. This can be set to the forward-looking period that suits the manufacturer. High volume/low value items are usually set to fewer months than higher value equipment. The benefits of interacting with the leasing company's data can only be derived if there is a good history of transacting leases together. The higher the leasing company's 'penetration' into the manufacturer's sales, the more benefits are unlocked.

Top quality benefits from this are, for instance:
- Good control of the situation.
- There is a valid reason to contact the Customer.
- A prompt can be presented to the Customer such as

– Now you're approaching maturity of the contract, what are your intentions regarding replacing or upgrading the original equipment?

- If the lease does not permit ownership at the end of term, a decision must be made by the Customer in good time about returning or replacing the equipment in good working order.

- If the lease includes a Residual Value, either the leasing company or the manufacturer could have the opportunity to re-market the equipment or re-lease it to a third party. A new profit opportunity becomes available, provided the residual value (originally set some years ago) is still viable in the used equipment market. This directly aids 'Circularity' credentials. If things have adversely impacted that residual value, there is a likelihood that a loss will be incurred. It is vital that the manufacturer and leasing company can rely on these predicted values otherwise financial disaster can result.

- The manufacturer is able to create efficiencies within their lean production schedules and procurement processes.

- Other suppliers can be locked out of this process because they will not know the accurate end date of the lease. The manufacturer is therefore in prime position to initiate a fresh replacement transaction.

If the manufacturer and leasing company are collaborating very closely, there is even more to explore by combining data sets, especially in the advent of telematics.

The IT System

In the meanwhile, the IT systems in use at our fictional manufacturer, JENZZO, have been built up over the years and the prime functions are to aid design (CAD/CAM), manufacture, procurement and 'Just in Time' stock control, including spare parts for the aftermarket operation. It is a highly valued, even revered and competent system. The internal Finance Team place a great deal of reliance on its outputs so as to manage Finance 1 functions. They have been very influential in developing its overall architecture and exert primary control over the management of the system and the IT Team. Changes are understandably rigorously controlled and fairly slow as a result.

The Sales and Marketing Team are less fortunate. They operate using a few sub-systems but spreadsheets and even exercise books are known to be in use to record some fairly important records. This also goes for some of the Service Team work who compile off-line service work times, labour and travel costs, plus warranty details and claims.

We now enter the latest Project B Team meeting where Mike has outlined the above scenario including the lack of 'lead' information.

Todd and Sam seem a little perplexed about there being any concerns because the IT system that they helped to create seems to deliver most of what the company needs. Sam acknowledges that there have been odd times when two individuals have kept separate and contradictory spreadsheets containing service costs, labour rates, travel allowances etc covering the same machine model, but this is tolerated due to the need for an 'off-line workaround'. After all, spreadsheets are the way these things have always been done. They have yet to see the new and extensive eco-systems that telematics and CRM software will create.

Sylvia feels a little more privileged because in her role within C Leasing, there has been much more emphasis on the 'Point of Sale' (POS) and her iPad-based system. She has colleagues who work with other manufacturers, particularly in the automotive and agricultural sectors. Their machinery Configure, Price, Quote (CPQ) software is amongst the class leaders.

Amy feels a little envious of Sylvia's systems and is looking forward to the forthcoming installation of a new cloud-based Customer Relationship Management (CRM) software system especially to gain some important Customer and lead tracking capability.

She also thought of the new car she had bought recently and how she could research online before going to the dealership to discuss a possible deal with the sales staff. This was the third time she had used such a system over the past five years, and she remained impressed at the way that she could build up the complete specification of the car and get a value of the part-exchange vehicle that she would trade-in. As each change was made, a prominent monthly finance payment also changed, using a Personal Contract Purchase (PCP) lease. This was really useful because it was the most important thing to determine her ultimate decision as she already knew what she could, or wanted, to afford.

A PCP is a type of car leasing agreement that allows you to drive a new or used car with lower monthly payments than a standard lease, while also having the flexibility to upgrade, return, or keep the car at the end of the contract. It essentially breaks down the cost of the car into smaller monthly payments, with a final 'balloon' payment if you choose to own the vehicle.

Over the past two years, Amy had spoken about this several times to her line manager, Lindsay, the Sales and Marketing Director. In the past, Amy had also discussed a CPQ system directly with Charlie (CFO) but failed to get the point across that their global pricing and sales approach was still pretty much rooted in the 1980s, based on expressing capital cost and aftermarket add-ons to Customers, rather than using the more relevant issue of monthly or other periodic payment programmes. On that occasion, Charlie said to her that "I never personally use leasing and always pay cash for my [expensive] motor car" and Amy had quipped, rather too quickly before turning on her heels and walking off, "suppose you wanted to buy ten cars for your business!?".

Lindsay had also used a similar CPQ system to create a specification for a luxury car a year ago when considering leaving the company car scheme and take an allowance instead, but had been persuaded by Charlie to choose from a list put together on a Salary Sacrifice Scheme[1] that saved the company money and passed on some of the benefit to Lindsay.

The idea of investing in creating a CPQ system for JENZZO wasn't seen as a priority for Charlie and the

IT Team, especially while the company was spending so much on installing the cloud-based CRM system. Lindsay was reluctantly content with this pragmatic stance for the moment.

Charlie, Todd and Sam also placed great stock in a 'Competitor Product Performance Comparison' App called *JENZZOversus* that had been developed by the IT Team and a group of engineers. This clever tool enabled the Sales Team to discuss and display to Customers a variety of competitor products supported by competitor images and competitor assumed cash prices and identify where JENZZO products performed better than the competition. The idea was to tease out what the Customer felt about the JENZZO product versus the competitor and where the competitor specifications and performance were short of the mark versus JENZZO.

The words competitor or competition are destructive!

The system is really a specification, features and benefits App requiring constant investment in updates as JENZZO and competitor new models and specifications are introduced across the markets served. It has poor cost justification capability and had no onboard funding solution. Even if the Customer wades through the minutia, which is naturally of so much interest to the designers and engineers, *JENZZOversus* is still abandoning the Customer to talk to outside credit suppliers to work out the financing arrangements to see if a lease might suit their investment budget and cashflow. This is after a salesperson like Jake has been 'pinned up against the wall' about a deeply discounted cash price.

The words *competitor* or *competition* are so destructive! As can be seen from the parody description above, the competitor product performance comparison App does relatively little to support the JENNZO brand, but it does reinforce, in the minds of their own salespeople <u>and</u> their Customers, that there is major credence in considering other suppliers or other brands. We shouldn't reinforce names of these other entities. Salespeople end up psychologically on the back foot if they utter those words. 'Captain Paranoia' sits on their shoulders and keeps nagging away, "be afraid, be very afraid of *competitors*".

Furthermore, the clever JENNZOversus App goes as far as attempting to work out the Customer's Total Cost of Ownership (TCO) for JENZZO and **competitor** products.

TCO? – the Customer doesn't own the kit!

I've already mentioned that I'm not the most qualified Finance 1 person but is the App likely to know a Customer's depreciation regime or any tax incentives in play or cost of insurance or machine operator costs or Internal Rate of Return (IRR) expectations or myriad other unknowns? The App assumes that the Salesperson is negotiating directly with someone who knows all about the Customer's Finance 1 issues, but more often than not they will be negotiating with an operations manager who is excluded from such information – even an owner operator may have to take time to refer to their external Accountant about such things.

However, the biggest flaw in such Total Cost of Ownership calculators is that almost inevitably the equipment will be acquired via a lease. <u>TCO? – the Customer doesn't own the kit!</u>

Forgive me, I really do not like the term TCO and it patently does not belong in the usership world of Product-as-a-Service.

Now, back to Amy. Apparently she had not learnt her lesson from that incident with FCO Charlie a while ago and stood her ground again in another conversation, prompting her to offer a firm rebuttal and left Charlie with the statement that "Customers don't have a pile of cash left under the bed mattress, you know, to pay for JENZZO equipment – they all use finance!".

Needless to say, Charlie felt that Amy was out of order again and should be ignored on this occasion and probably in the future too. Sales volumes were pretty good and, okay, margins were being squeezed but the key ratios were acceptable in the Finance 1 world. Charlie also held a long-felt view that Customers were far too sophisticated to be led by leasing facilities and was not yet convinced that leasing went further than a really useful payment option for people who didn't have the money at the end of negotiations. Charlie felt that the features and benefits of JENZZO products were already providing strong Unique Selling Propositions (USPs) and forward order levels were acceptable – at the moment.

Charlie's true colours had begun to show, but the stern glare given to Amy in response to her outburst bore an element of uneasiness. The consequences of the tariff reset and Net Zero obligations coming down the tracks were at least not entirely lost on Charlie.

Summary & Resources

So, there we are, the idea of transforming the sales process within JENZZO via the emerging outputs from the Plan B Project Team were beginning to stall. Charlie held a powerful position and seemed to be the 'immoveable object', and the team were not yet anywhere near being an 'unstoppable force'. They seemed destined to rely on a competitor comparison TCO App and an incoming CRM as the total answer to modernise their sales process and help Lindsay with the big performance leap.

Mike would need to use his leadership, considerable dexterity and powers of persuasion to upset this internal inertia. We'll see the strategy improvements and suite of tactics that the Project B Team put together in the next chapters.

[1] *Salary Sacrifice Scheme*
https://www.rac.co.uk/business/news-advice/
advice-guides/salary-sacrifice

CHAPTER 11

Rubicon Powered Sales Transformation

The Plan B Team had begun to suffer from a typical middle-management miscomprehension that their special project would be understood and welcomed by all stakeholders within the business. Having encountered inertia from parts of senior management, they would have to re-think and come up with building a fresh and comprehensive strategy.

They would realise that they had not fully deployed some of the Business Transformation tools that had been examined earlier. They had not mobilised enough support or project budget from CEO, Nicky and no Board presentation had been made up to that point.

Mike had been on a few management development courses over the years and picked up some useful pointers from all kinds of places including:

- The Dale Carnegie Organisation[1] and Carnegie's famous book, 'How to Win Friends and Influence People'. He had also been on some of their enlightening courses.
- The ancient Chinese text 'The Art of War' by the successful General Sun Tzu. The insights are still taught in military academies across the world. The principles were made accessible for business use by Donald G. Krause in his book The Art of War for Executives[2]. (See Figure 16)

Learn to Fight	Show the Way
Do it Right	Know the Facts
Expect the Worst	Seize the Day
Burn the Bridges	Do it Better
Pull Together	Keep them Guessing

Figure 16: The Ten Sun Tzu Principles

- Nobel prize winner Daniel Kahneman's book, Thinking, Fast and Slow[3] describes how humans have two modes of thought: System 1 is fast, instinctive and emotional and System 2 is slower, more deliberate and more logical.

My System 2 probably spends an erroneous amount of time creating back-up logic for swift and instinctive decisions I make using System 1! I don't think I'm alone.

It was time for Mike to make some important moves. His first port of call was with CEO Nicky. They both agreed that in the changing external circumstances, the Company needed to boost its defences and simultaneously lay the foundations for growth beyond introducing the new Airport Tug. A pivot to providing advanced services was a major part of the answer.

Nicky recognised that JENZZO had a tradition of ploughing profit back into Research and Development (R&D), but this was almost always focused on new or upgraded equipment offerings like more environmentally compliant engine technology, health and safety features or an additional model in their range. Mike's idea of providing R&D funding for research into things like better Customer contracts or innovative Point of Sale facilities struck a chord with Nicky. This helped to understand that outcome-based deals with Customers would be a step forward.

Market tensions would still pose the same questions BUT the answers would be different.

Along with several industry players and Customer focus groups, Nicky was on the Board of an Environmental Task Force looking into how Green House Gas (GHG) emissions pressure points were going to push businesses onto new paths to hit Net Zero regardless of government policy.

During the meeting with Mike, the penny dropped that JENZZO's future offerings to Customers had to go beyond equipment performance guarantees and shift even further to embrace Net Zero guarantees too.

Market tensions would still pose the same questions BUT the answers in future would be different. The new answers (outcomes) that Customers would be seeking would go beyond the mere productive capacity of JENZZO equipment – it would grow to include how JENZZO's advanced services would provide enablement for the Customer to meet their own Net Zero obligations. This became the seminal moment for Mike when, as Churchill put it in December 1941, he could "sleep the sleep of the saved"[5]. Plan B would become the pivot for JENNZO to transform to providing Advanced Services rather than carry on with the tongue in cheek quip 'flog some gear, sell some parts and hope for some service contracts'.

Nicky agreed to provide Mike and the Plan B Project Team with sufficient budget to allow them to research and create the necessary dynamic within the business to have far-reaching long-term consequences. Nicky would also look to achieve consensus with Board colleagues and JENZZO's owners, but Mike would need to provide a steady flow of influential material to help Nicky make the progress they both needed. Nicky would need to co-ordinate appropriate internal communications to all JENNZO employees and facilitate open access to company Divisions and global representatives.

Mike left the meeting and was thrilled to let the Plan B Project Team know of the progress made. There would now be a phase of strenuous work.

The task facing Mike and the team was fivefold:
- Create a compelling Advanced Services proposition.
- Foster a wider sense of community and keep

stakeholders informed.
- Leverage influencers.
- Engage with external experts.
- Offer Customers early access and exclusive benefits using the Airport Tug as the initial Plan B product.

Over the coming weeks the Plan B Team became a full-time Project with members having temporarily (so they thought) dispensed with their day-to-day job responsibilities.

Their focus took them into topics that had hardly ever received attention within JENZZO such as 'Behavioural Economics', creation of POS Apps, forming a much deeper partnership with C Leasing, widening the scope of Telematics, devising an award-winning individual Performance Improvement Scorecard, novel sales incentives, market surveys, scaling up the new CRM system and bespoke the software to match the new services pivot. Production of a 'Killer Proposition Pack' for use with Customer prospects, sales training and coaching plus improved online presence were also keys to progress. One of the transformational assets would have to be development of a new consultative language or narrative to run alongside the new Advanced Services Contracts being drafted together with expert lawyers. A small example of what that new language would look like was used earlier by Jake in his second scenario with the XP31 enquiry.

Rubicon Techniques

There follows a series of detailed examples aiding the high-speed progress of the Plan B Project mission:

Sales Enquiry – Scenario 3

JENNZO have now formed a closer and more formal relationship with C Leasing and Sylvia has been doing some coaching with the salespeople. Here's Jake running one of his new fortnightly structured four-hour canvassing sessions, taking the initiative with a prospect on an outbound sales prospecting call. He's noticed from combining his Rubicon Recency, Frequency, Profitability (RFP) table plus the C Leasing 'N Months to run' data, that a Customer called Import Export Metals Co are 47 months through their 60-month lease on an XP31 machine.

"Hi Françoise," says Jake to the Customer, "I'm phoning about the XP31 that I seem to remember you leased around four years ago. I've got some good news for you, we've just launched the XP32."

"How much is it?" says Françoise who is in charge of operations for the Customer.

Jake fires back: "Well, just remind me how much are you paying per month at the moment?" Jake has the number in front of him but wants Françoise to confirm the figure if possible.

"I remember about €1,200 a month," she replies.

"Fine," says Jake, "you know, I think I can get to around that figure on a new machine today! And you may have already heard that the new XP32 has some really interesting power regenerating features during its work cycles that reduce fuel consumption and cut down on those CO_2 emissions that I see you're having to publish nowadays in your annual reports. Our new telematics system is also making a big difference for Customers charting other cost savings too."

"OK, Jake, that sounds interesting, come and see me, I can't commit to any decision, but come and see me anyway," says Françoise.

What she doesn't know is that between Jake and Sylvia, and their Asset Management colleagues, they've already found a potential buyer for the used XP31. This will mean that C Leasing can manage the Residual Value position that they continue to hold on the XP31 during a second lease to a new Customer. As a result, JENZZO (and Jake) will receive some fresh revenue from re-selling the unit.

You will notice that we haven't yet perfected the Advanced Service Contract narrative, but we'll take a look at that in the following chapters including data from the new telematics system. It's becoming evident from combining data and applying rigour in its use it is capable of lifting sales momentum.

Through Syliva's coaching, Jake is beginning to use Consultative Sales Language (CSL) and Consultative Finance Language (CFL) by embedding so much more narrative in his approach that could explore and offer value to the Customer. It brings out many more engaging elements covering leasing, timing, control, using perspective, behavioural economics, telematics, storytelling and Net Zero.

He is also beginning to introduce circular economy principles from a second and maybe further usage of the machinery.

> *They are beginning to treat the*
> *C Leasing portfolio as an extension*
> *of JENZZO's used equipment stock*

Sylvia at C Leasing now hopes to have a fresh piece of new business on the used machine and wash out the original Residual Value her Asset Management Team set speculatively four years ago. Between them, they are beginning to treat the C Leasing portfolio as an extension of JENZZO's used equipment stock.

Behavioural Economics (BE)

There are huge quantities of scholarly and other literature published on this topic. They all provide valuable insights into the basic cognitive drivers people use that end up creating predictable biases and limitations that go on to explain why people can make irrational decisions. I cannot place myself in any scholarly position, but my experience has convinced me that organisations need to understand this profound topic in much better depth. It is extremely powerful in the way that individuals can be 'nudged' into making decisions – both good and bad.

One of the masters of BE science was Daniel Khaneman who was an Israeli-American psychologist best known for his work on the psychology of judgment and decision-making as well as behavioural economics, for which he was awarded the 2002 Nobel Memorial Prize in Economic Sciences together with Vernon L. Smith. His book *Thinking, Fast and Slow* has become a BE bible.

BE explains the complex background to the economic decisions that people make

Using this knowledge, firms can place BE at the forefront of sales and marketing strategy and Customer interactions. The place where my interest stems from is based on two key points of intrigue.

The first is recognising that when casual shoppers walk into say, a clothes shop – most aisle wanderers will not be conscious of the professional psychology that has been applied to the layout of the store, the location of the goods and the positioning within shelving, lighting, decor and position of check-out desks. A fortune will have been spent on attempting to pre-condition potential Customers before they even glance at or pick up an item to examine. Why then do many equipment manufacturers ignore the same psychology within their own sales process?

My second interest is the impact of making goods appear genuinely more affordable by using a properly integrated sales-aid finance offer to soften the Customer's human DNA-induced response of the price objection. The human will automatically create that mental price objection so why help it land there in the first place by displaying a bald cash price, especially without some other conditioning or perspective factor offering a positive comparison to something else?

The following sections shines a tiny light on how BE can explain the complex background to the economic decisions that people make and these can be very different to what general economic theory would expect. Theory assumes that people would have the right information about all relevant options at hand, and make a decision assessed on logical interrogation of that information in a selfish way that disregards the impact on other entities. In practice, people (Customers) do not act in this expected way. BE challenges this orthodoxy and explains how gaps can happen through non-logical factors like emotion, past experience or without having or understanding all the necessary information. (See Figure 17)

Firms that have a good understanding of BE can help to achieve better outcomes for Customers that contribute to longer-term relationships because of better decisions being made at the start of any negotiation. Of course, BE techniques can be misused, but that is not the purpose within this book beyond improving value for money sales margins (designed to achieve a win/win for both parties).

This combination of understanding and managing positive deployment of BE can lead to better 'Customer-centric' outcomes, but does require intensive training at all levels within the firm to ensure that product design, sales, marketing and service strategies focus on building and maintaining trust and thus build space and enablement for trading advantage. We can take a deeper look at the examples.

BE Examples

Price Anchoring	Creates imprints in our minds that go on to form reference points when making decisions.
Loss Aversion	The tendency for people to feel the pain of a loss more strongly than the pleasure of an equivalent gain.
Change Aversion	A lack of information and sticking to the status quo are two factors which highly influence people to act irrationally.
Present Bias	People value satisfaction in the present more than satisfaction in the future – and as such will make decisions which benefit them greater in the present.
Less Choice More Participation	When presented with too many options, people find it harder to make a decision due to being unable to evaluate and compare all the choices.
Endowment Effect	Loss aversion contributes to the endowment effect, where people value something they own more than they would if they didn't own it.

Figure 17: BE Examples

Price Anchoring

Value is often set by anchors or imprints in our minds which we then use as mental reference points when making decisions. An anchor is any aspect of the environment that has no direct relevance to a decision but that nonetheless affects people's judgments. Once an idea or a value is firmly anchored in someone's mind it can lead to automatic decisions and behaviours. For me, this generates another picture of Captain Paranoia sitting on a decision maker's shoulder nagging away at the perspective of the actual offer versus the Anchored Price – remember the impact of Jake's 115 number.

Our brain is biased towards making fast, but sometimes flawed, decisions

A BBC *Horizon* (2014) programme 'How You Really Make Decisions'[4] gave a masterly insight into many aspects of Behavioural Economics. It featured Daniel Khaneman with input from Dan Airely (another BE expert from Duke University in North Carolina). I strongly recommend that readers watch the programme. It majors on how our brain is biased towards making fast, but sometimes flawed, decisions using a kind of autopilot – 'System 1', which conducts most of the driving of our thoughts that form our immediate opinions. The programme goes onto to describe 'System 2' which deals with our rational thoughts and logic and is conditioned to be clever, but is lazy.

The clip between 22:25 and 26:00 shows compelling evidence about why price anchoring should be deployed in sales negotiations.

It involves random individuals on a London street being invited to place a price on a bottle of nice champagne but first they are asked to draw a numbered ping pong ball from a bag containing 100 ping pong balls.

They think that their slow and rational System 2 will choose a well-considered price for the bottle, but this will be hijacked by the number on the ball. The first set of people choose a ball but the all the balls have been rigged – they are all numbered 10. The second group are presented with an identical scenario but the number on their ping pong balls is also rigged as 65.

When asked about the price they would offer for the champagne, the first group respond with a low price between £7 and £20. The second group offer between £40 and £80. Both groups have been nudged into a figure by nothing more than a number on a ping pong ball. It's powerful stuff!

System 2 generally involves itself towards ratifying the quick decisions made by system 1 and therefore bolsters our biases. If we were to try to make all of life's decisions by using System 2, we would be driven mad – perhaps you know individuals who try to do this?

Loss Aversion

People are generally more motivated to avoid losses than to acquire gains of an equal size. This means the feeling of losing something resonates more than the feeling of gaining something of the same value. Also known as the 'pain of loss', it can significantly influence decision-making and actions in various contexts, including business strategies, performance management and sales techniques.

Loss aversion is therefore a powerful psychological phenomenon

A simple marketing approach is to place a short timescale onto a sales promotion. For instance, a zero or low-rate finance scheme may have a short end date to create a 'call to action' from targeted Customers, fostering the idea that they will lose out if they do not commit to an offer by the set date. This may also deflect some pressure on a demand for extra discount on the product's cash price.

Some organisations have used this effect within their internal incentive programmes by creating a rewards account for a salesperson set at an initial value. Where targets are not met, debits are made to the account which drives an increase in effort to prevent further diminishing of the remaining rewards pot. In some cases, this is a more powerful motivation technique than amounts accumulating in a reward account.

Loss aversion is therefore a powerful psychological phenomenon that shapes decisions and behaviours. Understanding it can help create strategies to ensure Customers make more informed choices and avoid being influenced by the natural focus on potential losses over gains.

Change Aversion

This involves the human tendency to resist change, preferring the status quo or the default option. This resistance is often linked to loss aversion, where individuals feel the pain of a loss more strongly than the pleasure of an equivalent gain. Change aversion can also be influenced by factors like status quo bias, where people favour what they already have or are accustomed to, and inertia, which makes it easier to stick with the default option.

This behaviour is sometimes the reason why Customers stick to what they know, even though circumstances may change over time and undermine the reasoning for their position.

By way of example, I've seen businesses continue to use simple leases to fund huge amounts of equipment because the Customer liked the idea of seeing large fixed asset values in their balance sheet, giving the impression of their own stature. Of course, they have to ignore the large amount of debt to support the value of the assets to make this self-contentment work. Indeed, certain alternative funding methods have often been used by other firms to minimise the value of assets (and related debt) on balance sheets, and this has provided benefits to be more conscious of managing cash and returns thereby making themselves perhaps more profitable. The change to emphasising the profit figure for these firms was therefore the overriding (and probably the most salient) sense of contentment versus the size of the pool of assets held to achieve it.

Businesses can use change aversion to their advantage by framing choices in a way that emphasises the potential loss of the current option to create 'safe' conditions for the Customer to move from one operational scenario to another more beneficial one.

Present Bias

Rational economic behaviour would suggest that Customers will make decisions based on how much they benefit their businesses over the entire duration of a project or the firm in general. However, even hard-nosed businesspeople can respond to urges for immediate gratification, even if this results in a smaller overall reward. This is probably one of the drivers of so much short-termism in commerce today. Firms are regularly under pressure from stakeholders to show growth in short-term returns rather than performing to a longer-term strategy that involves patience when investing in new strategies or products.

When putting offers, propositions or ideas to Customers, present bias should be considered or structured to take this into account. This is also particularly important when presenting ideas internally about transforming into a servitization business model where profits from sales of product become entwined with profits from advanced services earned over the lifetime of a product. This can have the effect of temporarily dampening profitability in the short-term but enhancing longer-term returns together with locking in a Customer, thus creating a longer-term relationship and income stream based on mutual benefits.

Less Choice More Participation

We see this in everyday life when presented with too much choice in a restaurant – creating more choice can often lead to less effective overall decision making. Customers can sometimes be time poor and want to get on with more important matters. In this case, socialising with fellow diners.

The ultimate effect is 'Choice Overload' leading to paralysis of decision making

The same can happen with manufacturer 'menu' based service packages that can develop to have too many choices. This is in part caused by the desire to split packages to help cost-justify various choices, but in its wake, leaves a bewildering list of choices. The ultimate effect is 'Choice Overload' leading to paralysis of decision making and lower take-up.

Slimming down options and attending to pricing strategies could help Customers to make the most suitable decision to meet their particular circumstances. Other issues include things like decision fatigue and increased regret, where Customers may regret their decision because they begin to think about the plethora of alternatives they didn't choose.

Creating a default option can help a Customer to make a decision because when presented with multiple choices it requires the least effort and is often perceived as the safer or recommended choice.

Endowment Effect

This is quite a powerful influence over how Customers value assets that they own and is often the cause of failed negotiations. This bias occurs because Customers place an unreasonable or irrational value on an owned asset during discussions, meaning they are unwilling to part with it at a price that others would regard as fair.

This could be based on an emotional or symbolic attachment – maybe the asset was the first one of its type acquired for the business or the amount of effort that has been previously expended to make it work properly.

I have seen this in action where businesspeople have decided not to move with changed circumstances because an old and faithful trading model has produced good results in the past – Kodak springs to mind.

The above examples are a limited BE selection but provide some useful background on the skills needed to shift people and firms from one position or paradigm to another. This has importance beyond dealing with Customers and has direct relevance to the power of persuasion involved with internal business transformation.

"Move from needing to do what we
like to liking what we need to do"

The JENNZO Plan B Project Team will benefit from understanding some of these BE basics. In particular, they will have to create internal and external motivations to "move from needing to do what we like to liking what we need to do".

Consultative Finance Language (CFL) – Introduction

Most of my career has been spent in a sales-aid environment. I sometimes felt as if it was part of a 40-year mission to constantly influence equipment sales processes, operated by a wide variety of manufacturers and dealers both large and small, who were entrenched in a cash price dominated sales model coupled to subordinated after-sales services. It was very apparent that the salespeople who used finance as a sales-aid rather than just a payment option at the end of negotiations sold more equipment, earned more money and improved margins (by taking some pressure off cash price objections and improving cost justification).

My observation with servitization is that the sales process becomes almost back-to-front with little demarcation between sales and services. They both become shape-shifted and amalgamated within the overall sales process revolving around selling Advanced Services based on equipment that becomes treated like an enabling platform. This is a difficult change for sales and service people to make.

Salespeople frequently focus on features and benefits and especially cash prices as almost the only negotiating tools. The change needs to be grasped in a world where domestic manufacturers are under increasing threat from low-cost/high quality suppliers – the price war becomes almost unwinnable.

Service people are committed to fixing faults but often miss opportunities to carry out preventative maintenance when they respond to a problem during the same visit. This is either a competence matter or the belief that the Customer will not respond well to another inconvenience or the repair needs to be classed as another chargeable fix. Obviously within servitization, the service personnel would have to be motivated to conduct a swift secondary repair because it will be the service provider who usually foots the bill. Although hopefully budgeted within the Advanced Services contract, the manufacturer faces the cost burden of every service, maintenance and repair activity. Poor use of the equipment or outright abuse are another matter.

Trading advantage can no longer be based on features and benefits and cash price discounting; it has to come from other areas.

There are many components and challenges in achieving this, and the following section is devoted to one vital part of the servitization transformation, which is the integration of sales-aid finance into the Customer proposition.

'helping to make a deal work'

Firstly, I have to admit that the word 'Finance' can be a turn off for most equipment salespeople. In the context of the equipment sales world, it smacks of having to master accountancy which is anathema to the career path chosen. The idea of 'wearing two heads' can sometimes be resented; however, with servitization, the Salesperson has to become a hydra – the many headed beast from Greek mythology!

We can't change the word 'Finance', but we can help with a better definition which is 'helping to make a deal work'. This is accomplished by creating a better business case to help the Customer to cost justify an investment.

General Prospecting

Before any deal is concluded, there has to be a good beginning. My experience tells me that many Salespeople can have a tendency to shrug off the responsibility of Customer/deal prospecting. They prefer to pick up a warm lead originated from elsewhere and thus become the 'deal warrior' – the deal negotiator and closer. This is not really performing the full responsibility of the role, and it is compounded by Sales Management if they do not measure prospecting performance or even require it as part of the job.

Capital goods manufacturers, in particular, cannot rely entirely on brand presence and promotion to generate flows of good quality, qualified leads. Customers still expect to have personal contact with suppliers, and that means face-to-face or supported by regular telephone contact.

I found that if there was a change in Sales personnel covering a particular region, it could take up to six months of intensive canvassing, supported by marketing activities and line management resources to establish the new individual with Customers in such a way that productivity was restored back to previous levels. That was quite a harsh and expensive lesson, especially if the replacement individual was of poor calibre or did not have the motivation required. A loss of Customer base is an expensive thing to recover. First class recruitment processes to put in place the correct talent search parameters are obviously key to avoiding the on-going risk of changes in representation on the ground.

> *A lack of qualified leads will often go*
> *on to stimulate desperate, expensive*
> *and wasteful reactions.*

As mentioned earlier, many would recognise that a Business to Business (B2B) model cannot sit back and rely on e-commerce, search engines, social media, emails etc to be the oxygen of their pipelines. A lack of qualified leads will often go on to stimulate desperate, expensive and wasteful reactions.

Using Customer segmentation could identify useful instances where Customers are 'Collaborators' or 'Brand Addicts', which infers that they would be committed to making purchases almost regardless of local representation. If a salesperson becomes over-reliant on these sources, there is a risk that other potential Customers are being ignored. One way to avoid this is to ask the question "what are we paying sales commissions for on such accounts?". Modifying sales commission payments on accounts identified in such segments could realign prospecting priorities.

The Rubicon Recency/Frequency/Profitability (RFP) table comes into its own here and also provides feedback on the rate and quality of contact being sustained, either in person or through e-commerce.

This may sound like a quaint throwback to the past, but I insisted on regular RFP-based mandatory canvassing sessions with each sales agent recording outcomes of: No Contact, Quality Contact, New Proposal, New Appointment. The sessions were required to take place for four hours every second and third Tuesday in a month. Mondays and Fridays were avoided because of Customers being unlikely to take calls seriously and the same with the first and last weeks of each month due to business pressures. Tuesday mornings proved to be the ideal time.

The activities of each participant (internal and external Sales representatives) had the number of their calls and outcomes displayed for all staff to view on a real-time basis. This promoted a competitive and fun spirit between participants and also reminded all staff of the efforts being made to win business to pay our salaries! This carried on even throughout the financial crisis 2008-2014 to good effect. Each session required a target of 30 calls. Sales veterans reported surprisingly positive outcomes and came to see the sessions as good business generators.

Eventually the metrics revealed that for every ten calls a new proposal was generated. Every 20 calls generated a fresh and profitable transaction – there could be little argument about the efficacy of this regime.

The regular canvassing was a million miles away from 'Search Engine Optimisation' (SEO) and myriad other online new business attractors. The RFP was invaluable in this activity.

Training & Coaching

Can we take an honest look at training and coaching for modern sales skills? I'm not talking DEI or fire safety here, I mean on genuine honing of skills to be used face-to-face or on the phone with sophisticated buyers who may well have received sophisticated buyer training themselves.

How much has been invested in modern sales training compared to say capital investment in machine tools, production lines, new products, regulatory compliance, hygiene maintenance, health and safety?

What is the single biggest component that generates wealth? Brand, patents, reputation, previous experience, reliability, durability, re-sale value are incredibly and traditionally important, but the world is changing fast. New market entrants are appearing at break-neck speed. New technologies are shaking old foundations. Low-cost/high quality manufacturing regions are offering unprecedented challenge to domestic manufacturers.

Investing in quality sales coaching
inspires professionals

Investing in quality sales coaching inspires professionals to do better, especially for high value capital goods. Ultimately it is usually people meeting people that will achieve a mutually satisfactory sale or relationship. How much has been invested in sales process optimisation to improve the chances of continuous success?

One important question arises: does any of the sales

training or coaching that may have been taking place lack real focus on financial solutions that helps salespeople translate values financially in these tough economic times? It is an established fact that in tough times, power sponsorship for investments made by firms moves away from their operational people to their finance people and so sales propositions have to be shaped to appeal to these power sponsors within a prospective Customer. This area will be covered in more detail shortly.

Metrics

Meanwhile, what metrics are being routinely reviewed to identify conversions, low average order values, high discounts, sub-optimal up-selling and low 'bundling', poor account management or individuals chasing quantity instead of quality? How is time-management instilled and how is oversight conducted to spot individuals or teams losing motivation or skills to surpass targets?

Creating High Performers

High rewards can be confused with high performers. It's not unusual to find individuals receiving high rewards but delivering mediocre results. Some of the reasons behind this include personality, assumed reputations, previous achievements, long service, acquired position, demand for equivalence and recognition. These can skew reality over time and create a false impression and become undermined by other rising stars.

The truth is that those rising stars have become competent, qualified and confident individuals and are achieving great things. They don't happen by chance, they happen by change. That change is probably part of a wider plan which will be covered in the Rubicon Performance Management Chapter but for now, there are five key components for successful high performers:

- Comprehensive product knowledge and competence to a desired level before they start.
- Real knowledge of integrating financial solutions in the sales process and their use in cost justification and the business case.
- Modern sales/helping Customers to buy competence – learned and practised at start level.
- Total competence in planning and managing sales activities with special focus on prospecting and pipeline management. This involves great forecasting competency and conversion probability judgement.
- Motivation and attitude assessment to ensure there is a will to win and desire for self-improvement meaning a desire to learn.

A further mention here of integrating financial solutions. When Sales-Aid Finance is used and positioned correctly, it is an incentive to help open, manage and close a sale. It therefore needs to be positioned at the start of negotiations. Equipment salespeople should not have specialist finance people sweep up behind them – it's too late.

Remember the mental picture of trying to coax a horse onto a trailer by dangling the carrot at the rear end of that negotiation? – it is plainly wrong. The draw or lure needs to be at the front.

JENZZO Sales-Aid Finance – Decision Time

It was an important day for Mike, the project leader and Sylvia from (C Leasing). They were to make a presentation to a JENZZO Board Meeting and the agenda included a lengthy slot covering a proposal to create a more formal relationship with C Leasing. Sylvia was accompanied by her Colaborar Bank (C Bank) Country VP, Amiya.

The meeting included the Board Members: Chair Lee, CEO Nicky, Sales Director Lindsay, CFO Charlie, COO Robin and Service Director Nico plus the Plan B representatives. The meeting was intended to decide what type of relationship would be formed. (See Figure 18)

Amiya undertook the 'ice-beaker' and confirmed how C Bank could enter into a new arrangement beyond the relatively informal relationship that had been taking place. C Bank had coverage in Western Europe, and was strong in Central and South America plus the Philippines and had representation in Oceana and some Gulf States.

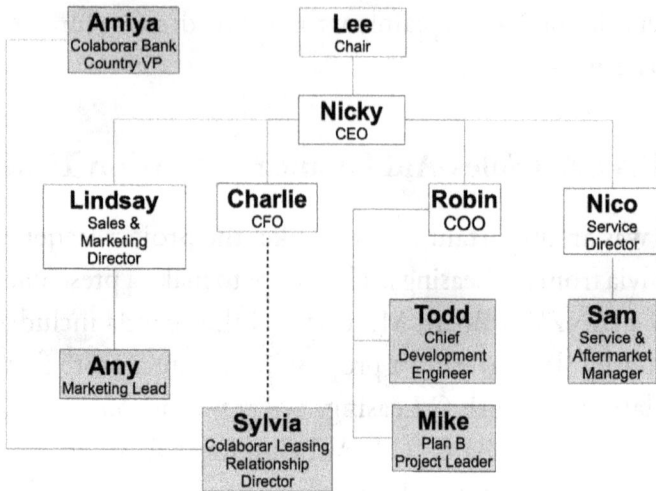

Figure 18: The Board Meeting Attendees

Mike and Sylvia had already laid the foundation for JENZZO to go ahead with a more formal relationship with C Leasing by means of a paper circulated to the Board Meeting participants outlining the benefits of linking to the large existing business portfolio held by C Leasing. These included the following:

- A dedicated Relationship Manager who would be responsible for all interactions with C Leasing and the broader C Bank organisation.
- C Bank would co-ordinate all Regulatory matters, particularly in the start-up phase. A suite of reports would be needed on a monthly basis.
- Analysis of the C Leasing Customer portfolio for possible JENZZO future target opportunities.
- Unlocking Tools like 'N' Months to run data on appropriate C Leasing deals reaching maturity.

- Access to a C Leasing tool called DealRadar which uses Artificial Intelligence to create sample propositions for Customers based on JENZZO pricing and predicted resale values of existing kit held on the C Leasing portfolio in advance of existing lease maturities.
- Close collaboration on developing the powerful C Leasing POS IT & Apps based on 5G enabled tablets called *Sprinter*.
- Access to the online C Leasing deal proposal system via an interface with the new cloud-based CRM so that pipeline data was keyed only once.

Vendor Model

The first model proposed involved a fairly standard 'Vendor' arrangement whereby C Leasing would become a formal partner of JENZZO and adopt the name Colaborar Leasing trading as JENZZO Advanced Services Contracts (JENZZO ASC). The arrangement would initially have selected C Leasing staff acting as JENZZO ASC representatives across C Bank's territories. C Leasing would provide 'back office' support to handle new business proposals and credit checking together with Anti-Money Laundering and many associated regulatory checks. Customer repayments and arrears handling would be administered and all 'Finance 1' accounting would be controlled by C Bank.

A small dedicated team within JENZZO HQ would be formed to act as the interface between both parties and

C Leasing's IT systems would form the backbone of proposal and transaction management. Some excellent Point of Sale (POS) Apps were available, from Configuring, Pricing and Quotations (CPQ), going on to record proposed Customer transaction details. Other manufacturers with whom C Leasing provided Vendor services were beginning to experiment with APIs to allow for flows of data to and from C Leasing regarding telematics information. Most of the cost of this development work was being borne by the vendor partners. Some of C Leasing's core systems were based on legacy IT resources and could be expensive to upgrade.

The money to be lent to Customers would come from C Bank at fairly competitive rates and all the lease profits would be due to C leasing in consideration of the risks being taken. Similar services would be available across C Leasing's markets and take into account local regulations and taxes etc.

JENZZO products would be sold to JENZZO ASC, causing the transaction to be classed under accounting rules as a clean deal so that turnover and profit could be booked immediately by JENZZO.

On the ground, staff training and joint special promotional activity could be provided by C Leasing. C Bank was content to allow certain residual values to be taken by C Leasing on new equipment, but it would be rigorously controlled and fairly inflexible. Guaranteed buy-backs could be called for from JENZZO if C Leasing thought the values too risky compared to their assessment of future valuations. This would mean that a 'contingent liability' would be created on the JENZZO balance sheet, thus defeating some of the impact of declaring a clean sale in the first place. Residual Risk Sharing would be considered on a deal-by-deal basis. This could have serious implications if Mike and the Plan B Team were to pursue servitization where, potentially, every sale would require a meaningful residual value to be struck. This could also impact the objective of creating second life sales of products.

C Leasing also had vendor relations with other manufacturers but fortunately had only limited cross-over with JENZZO product lines – at the moment. The vendor model would have a good degree of dedication to JENZZO interests, but the other relationships would also be served.

Joint Venture (JV) Model

A second, fairly rare, model was presented whereby both parties would form a Joint Venture company, still called JENZZO ASC, owned jointly by both parties on a suggested 75%:25% basis with the bank holding the majority share. In this way, JENZZO would be selling its products to a business designated as a direct subsidiary of the bank, enabling JENZZO to again class the sale as a clean transaction under accountancy rules, and book the turnover and profit immediately. Profits (or losses) made each year by the JV could be retained or shared proportionately between the shareholders with agreed surpluses being paid as dividends.

More resources would be needed to establish this model, especially if JVs were to be formed in multiple regions, and although C Bank would be providing funding at almost similar levels of interest (treasury) rates to its internal group companies, there would be a separate management charge levied on the JV, especially during the formative phase while the JV was closely supported by C Leasing and until suitable profit flows could be seen in the years to come to enable tangible dividends to be paid to both shareholders.

A CEO of the JV and various other management and administration roles would have to be put into place. There would be a burden of regulatory controls and oversight from the bank to ensure that its interests were being controlled properly within the JV.

The JV would be completely dedicated to JENZZO sales

There was, however, an opportunity for the talented JENZZO IT Team to do some of their own development on POS Apps linking to the incoming cloud-based CRM software meaning that they would not have to wait every time for the bank's systems to deliver fairly large or even small bespoke development projects. The JV would be completely dedicated to JENZZO sales and its transformation effort.

Retaining profits in the business would help build up capital not only to shield both parties from unlikely trading losses but also eventually underpin the residual value risks taken should equipment not reach predicted secondary values in later years. Interestingly, any residual values incorporated into Advanced Services Contracts would rest on the JV balance sheet with any recorded loss or profit on re-sale being absorbed by the JV company, away from JENZZO Group accounts. Placing Residual Values in the JV would be permitted up to certain limits but under strict scrutiny by C Bank.

At this point, the Chairperson, Lee, thanked Mike and Sylvia and the Plan B Team for their hard work in placing the shareholders in a position to discuss important and far-reaching decisions which would need to take place privately with Amiya.

Lee also confirmed that the family owners of JENZZO were now convinced, because of the Plan B progress, that the business could no longer rely on the old 'Sales and After Market Model' and 'Advanced Services' would have to form the main thrust of their future trade. Mike, Sylvia and the team were feeling very pleased with what they had heard.

The behind-the-scenes discussions were very detailed. Both options were considered. The most complex issues concerned becoming prospective JV shareholders. The talks involved various 'Reserved Matters' to be controlled by the shareholders, such as who and how a CEO would be appointed (or exited). The value of the investment in shares or other capital support plus voting rights. Who would Chair this new entity? What to do in case of an irreparable breakdown between the shareholders. The cost of treasury funds, the level of the management fee, the level of support to be made available to the new JV CEO and Team.

Licensing the JENZZO name and registered trade-marks were important as were the needs of data protection, security and viability of data flows between the entities.

All of these matters would need to be documented for all regions that JV arrangements were to cover.

The lawyers would become richer and the Finance 1 Team would, no doubt, sigh somewhat at their forthcoming involvement in accommodating the Finance 2 venture.

In due course, Mike and the Plan B Team would find out which option was selected to provide JENZZO with the foundation to enable their strategic sales transformation.

Summary & Resources

In this chapter we've added considerable weight to the faltering Sales Transformation we met in the preceding chapter.

The 'Rubicon' supercharging has been achieved by digging into personal resilience and making a fight for the transition away from the simple traditional model of sales and aftermarket. Mike has made progress with the CEO and had resources allocated.

One of the most helpful moves was to explain about the need to incorporate Behavioural Economics as a strong catalyst to be included in future decision making and training. We moved this into recognising the need to develop a more formalised relationship with an asset finance provider to help create some of those BE perspectives. JENZZO Group was going to end up with a formal sales-aid finance arrangement.

Using BE coupled with sales-aid finance materials and infrastructure plus metrics gave fresh impetus to sales staff carrying out their own canvassing to generate quality leads.

Firms need to monitor deployment of BE techniques as part of any interaction with Customers to ensure positive outcomes.

[1] *How to Win Friends and Influence People*
Dale Carnegie. Ebury Publishing.
ISBN: 9780091906818.
Dale Carnegie Organisation
www.dalecarnegie.com/en-gb

[2] *Sun Tzu, The Art of War Foe Executives*
Donald G Krause, John Murray Press.
ISBN: 9781857881318

[3] *Thinking, Fast and Slow*
Daniel Kahneman. Penguin Books.
ISBN: 9780141033570

[4] *'How You Really Make Decisions'*
A BBC *Horizon* (2014) programme
https://www.dailymotion.com/video/x3q4alx

[5] "Sleep the sleep of the saved" - Churchill quote, See:
https://winstonchurchill.org/publications/churchill-bulletin/
bullertin-162-dec-2021/pearl-harbor/

CHAPTER 12

Consultative Finance Language (CFL)

This is where we combine the efforts of sales transformation, behavioural economics, sales-aid finance and an important grade of sales vocabulary.

We're going to expand on Jake's rudimentary examples of reshaping a negotiation around cash price to encompass a range of questions and responses that can become powerful means of persuasion when selling capital equipment. We're still not at the stage of polishing the techniques needed when negotiating advanced services, but this chapter provides the underpinning or platform for that task.

It's extremely difficult to move directly from negotiating on a cash price sale and aftermarket basis into a consultative advanced service basis without first understanding the preliminary ground rules.

Consultative Finance Language (CFL) takes time to master and so practice is essential. Some salespeople will not like the challenge and will baulk at it. Some people need to do what they like rather than like what they need to do.

Some people need to do what they like rather than like what they need to do

This category of person will have a strong belief in their lengthy, tried and tested, sales experience. They may insist that their ten or 20 years of experience cannot be ignored. However honourable it may be to recognise time served in very demanding frontline sales duties, it can sometimes disguise one year's experience repeated ten or 20 times. It will not be possible to reorientate everyone and it is here where we have to remember Jake's first shot at the Customer enquiry. He was not able to frame his response properly to the incoming enquiry and the Customer went away thinking that acquiring the XP31 machine was too expensive. If the Customer received the same response from other suppliers of similar machines, they would also likely stall their decision to invest because they had been left with no perspective of affordability or justification of the cost. They have been left alone to self-justify. Of course, this may be perfectly possible but which supplier are they now going to choose – JENZZO or another brand? Some important control of the sale has been lost.

Upgrading selling skills is not based on flushing out wrong practice for all to see, it's about making things better in a 'no fear' way. A quote, often attributed to Einstein is relevant here *"insanity is doing the same thing over and over again and expecting different results"*. The thing to keep in mind is the impact on the firm's bottom line if three percent more deals were done each quarter per salesperson or an extra 3% margin achieved on each transaction.

Exploring CFL

We should not send salespeople to appointments to negotiate on our behalf with sophisticated buyers without adequate coaching. The cost of this neglect can be seen in underperforming volumes, deep discounting behaviour and anxiety. Lack of up-selling and cross-selling will be evident – if sales management cares to look.

Given that finance options are provided at almost every Point of Sale in the 21st Century, it is simply not right to continue to visit the Customer in this modern age without taking the money with you.

I never regarded myself as 'selling finance' – I believed that I was using finance to help Customers to buy

I've had my share of debates with salespeople who feel that their sophisticated buyer 'would never fall for that treatment' on a large capital item and yet it has become second nature with the general public about how cars are sold on finance involving low entry deposit, affordable monthly payments and a large payment due at the end, usually covered by the underlying residual value of the car – a PCP lease. Employees and even high-flying sophisticated directors of firms use this in a high proportion of car sales in the UK – so much for the disdain of 'sophisticated' buyers. If this is such a universal technique, how come so many firms ignore it when it comes to selling their own equipment? It is probably the lack of sophistication in the seller's approach that causes their sales-aid phobia.

An important point here is that I never regarded myself as 'selling finance' – I believed that I was using finance to help Customers to buy equipment.

> *Learning how to express value over time should become second nature*

The following statements, phrases, questions and responses may sound fairly puerile but try to put this to one side. The phrases have been honed from serious study, and I've witnessed how useful the outcomes can be from adopting this into natural vocabulary. Learning how to express value over time should become second nature.

Handling Price

We've already encountered Jake's progress from relying on cash price to using periodic payments to then comparing an outstanding lease deal, so let's see what other conversational tools can be used.

- We already know that a Customer is bound to ask for a cash price discount. Why do we set up that trigger moment? Hardly anyone ever says straight away "that's a real bargain!".
- Can we help the Customer to see the difference

that justifies the cost? Are they just looking to be convinced?

- Leading with cash price simply invites a direct comparison with another supplier. This makes it an uphill struggle to defend any premium.

- The futility of negotiating on cash price is amply demonstrated when we look at how the Customer will fund the purchase. The Customer normally looks to invest in new equipment because they either want to make more money or save costs. Not many Customers have large sums of cash waiting to be employed, but even if they did, their investment would be viewed against the returns expected over time. The equipment would incur depreciation, and we can use this to compare to a leasing deal. The difference in a monthly or daily payment will not be great over, say, five years. Most firms will use a bank, leasing company or family funds – they borrow to invest.

- Most businesses that fail are those who run out of cash. They may be full of innovation and growth plans, but a cash-crunch can come out of nowhere. It therefore makes sense to use someone else's money to fund chunky equipment and retain cash to cope with everyday needs.

- Remember that using a finance comparator such as "only €5 a day" (over seven years at 240 working days per annum) will yield extra revenue of around €8,500 – upfront.

- Used the other way round, to hold out for that extra €5 a day, gives a platform to distinguish the performance or outcomes of our equipment versus another option – "for only €5 per day, you get XYZ".

- A good comparator can be found in talking through the expected utilisation levels. It's not really possible with an upfront cash price but it is relatively easy to do with periodic payments, almost to the point of working out a leasing or advanced services cost per working hour/cycle/pack.

Using Behavioural Economics – Examples

We learnt some basics earlier in the book and this is the point where we can convert some of that knowledge into dialogue.

- I can count on one hand how many Customers have cancelled a leasing deal once they have signed the lease because it is perceived as a solemn legal act. However, cancelling an order was unfortunately less of a barrier. It therefore makes sense to get a lease signed as early as possible.
- Special leasing schemes have a very important part to play because they can be a temporary offer requiring decisions to be made in a limited period. It makes sense to run a low-rate scheme (using part of the discount usually granted) to offer an attractive package. If cash price deep-discounts are a continuous feature of sales behaviour, how can better margins be secured? The Customer will appreciate that the special leasing deal is a limited offer – how many times can we recover from regular cash price discounting?

The Customer will remember the price for next time. The leasing deal can build in a higher price which becomes the new starting point next time.

- Phrases like "for another €5 per day, you can get a bigger, faster, more efficient unit" are easy to portray on a lease. Try that using an extra €8,500 on the cash price!

- Customers can be convinced to make a little more investment if the salesperson treats the lease as a running account utility alongside the main deal. For instance, "For only €X per day/week/month/pack/movement, I can add the XYZ accessory to your account *while we've got it open*".

- Before attempting to close a deal, it makes sense to talk in terms of approximate figures – being too explicit removes room for movement. This means being approximate and converting numbers into conversational and small denominations. Using "something like €x" per day/week/month/batch.

Spontaneity can add to our plan – not be the plan

Story Telling & Self Perception

Story telling is not about spinning untruths, it is about adding context and richness born out of real-life experience to enhance the authenticity of our discussions.

- Using the 'Rubicon Forcefield Analysis' mentioned earlier, we can plan for the type of narrative or stories to use during the negotiation. We do not need to leave this to chance or pressurise ourselves to come up with the right topics on the fly. Spontaneity can add to our plan – not be the plan.
- Can we find stories of similar situations where Customers benefited from the type of equipment or the lease or service option chosen?
- Can we demonstrate how this was done?
- I have a story to tell from many years ago. A good Customer and friend of mine was buying a large piece of equipment that would be a big advantage for his firm. At the time, I was in a position to sell Personal Protection Insurance (PPI) that would cover him in the case of an injury or even death, ensuring that his business could carry on and his family would be protected. The premium for the insurance cover was a lot of money, and I decided that I couldn't offer it, as in my own opinion, it didn't represent a good 'value for money' proposition even though it could be granted without a medical examination. We completed the lease without it. A few months later, I was talking socially with his wife, and she wished that such insurance cover was available because her husband had previously been rejected by other life assurance providers on health grounds. I was glad when the repayment period was completed successfully. It taught me a lesson not to let personal value perceptions interfere with business offers.

- Here's another story. I like to remind myself about polo style shirts – one has the logo of my favourite pub (a place that gives me regular pleasure), another carries the design of my favourite football team (a place that gives me regular disappointment). Both shirts will be hard wearing but one can be bought for €20 and lasts a lifetime, and the other for €100 and lasts maybe one season. I guess you and your Customers can relate to similar examples where they don't automatically go for the cheapest option. Some buying decisions are not rational!
- Items that we buy in our personal lives feel very important. If we're lucky, a house, a fancy car, super holiday and each may have an equivalent underlying monthly or daily cost. Even a small business could incur expenditure of €2,000 per day. Our personal experience is usually not on the same level as business expenses, and we should leave such thoughts outside a business meeting.

Convincing Vocabulary

Nothing beats doing the homework before contacting the Customer, but after that, how is it that some salespeople can enter negotiations in a smooth and confident way that puts the potential Customer at ease. I've seen them in action and they are masters in handling objections or tough questions and their responses never seem assertive or confrontational but are interpreted as helping to find a mutually satisfactory solution.

A good example is where the Customer goes quiet after being asked for the order. The rule is don't break the silence, wait and wait again. If it goes on too long it might help to say something like "I've known of many times when silence can mean consent, it feels like we should get on with things".

I've heard that objections can even go as far as the Customer saying "But I just don't like you!" – a quick response to break the tension might be: "Fine, I can understand that, do me a favour, try harder!" delivered with a grin – after all, there is little to lose in that situation.

It's a natural talent but they are characteristics that can be learnt – it's not magic. It takes effort, repetitive effort. Maybe by self-recording, especially in front of a mirror. Sometimes written down to aid the memory process. I've been involved in helping to produce audio recordings that can be listened to and memorised even when on the move, just like learning a new language.

Direct Sale Phrases

Some often forgotten easy one-liners to use on the phone or face-to-face go like this:
- I'm sure we can help, what have you done about this so far?
- To make sure this will work for both of us. I need to ask a few simple quick questions...
- Before you start shouting at me you know it will cost another few € a week for the XYZ ...
- Before I tell you about XYZ I need to ask a couple of

important questions...
- How much does this cost? Well that depends on how long you're keeping it for...
- It would be helpful if you could tell me...
- It would help me if you could give me an indication of how you measure payback...
- I guess it would help if we could cost justify the investment...
- We can put these in place at entry level instalments of something like €X to €Y per day...
- Think about it this way – I was with another Customer the other day... does that sound like the same decision you've got to make?
- Does that sound like it would be useful to you sometime?
- Of course you need to think about it. Let me summarise what there is to think about and I'll come back to you later...
- I'd like to let you know about some of these things sometime...
- And how does that work for you?
- I've been at JENZZO for 15 years. It's a good company otherwise I wouldn't be here [Use this as a strength value].
- I've a whole range of financial and advanced service solutions, most of which won't apply to your business, it would help me to explore your situation for a few minutes...
- If you do this then I can do that...
- It will be really nice or useful if you could talk me

through...
- The other brand is good. How's that working for you? What did you like about them? [You will learn about compromises]
- We need to do X and Y to take the next step?
- When taking on more equipment these days, a lot of Customers are telling me that they need to find ways to invest but also retain cash in their business for a rainy day...
- Now, let's see, these are the things you've told me you need. How do they rank in order of priority?
- If I can match all or even most of your needs, will we be in the right territory to go ahead? [pre-close]
- We've covered everything pretty well, all it takes is a signature on the dotted line and we're ready.

Influencer Sale Phrases

In many circumstances it may not be possible to speak to the real decision-maker and negotiations have to be conducted via an intermediary such as an Operations Manager.

In tough times, power sponsorship within businesses moves away from operational people to the finance people

It is an established fact that in tough times, power sponsorship within businesses moves away from operational people to the finance people and so offers have to be shaped to appeal to the power sponsors. In these circumstances, leading negotiations requires a modified CFL approach. We are now dealing with an influencer within the Customer's firm.

Sit alongside the influencer and use some easy one-liners that go like this:

- What's your firm's medium- to long-term vision?
- I'd really like to understand where you're going.
- At the moment is finance/risk management/Net Zero a top value around investments in equipment?
- Do 'upstairs' want to stop spending, reduce costs, minimise risk and measure financial impact?
- Tell me what do we or you need to do to make this happen?
- I guess the big challenge for you is getting the machine proposal agreed upstairs.
- Talk me through what criteria you apply to important decisions.
- We may be a few € a week more but you get a lot more with me and our company...
- What are the biggest decision drivers around the business right now?

Cross-Sell Phrases

As mentioned before, we should not assume that the Customer always prefers the cheapest option. Selling extra features should be related to this stance. Some one-liners go like this:

- So you're looking for this solution at €30 a day – how much do you think this will save you?
- It seems sensible to add XYZ for €x per day/pack/lift to maximise your return...
- Before we wrap this up why don't we look at this XYZ attachment for only €x per day/pack/cycle? We can pop this on our finance programme while I'm here...
- What do you think it's up to you? I can't make that decision for you...
- Has anyone told you about our new service plan?

The above CFL sections really just scratch the surface of sales encounters and are intended to stimulate thought about how prepared salespeople are to take on the challenge in fairly simple situations. For more complex and, perhaps, higher value capital sales, 'Know Your Customer' obviously takes on even greater importance, beyond the Rubicon Forcefield Analysis tool.

Killer Proposition Pack (KPP) – Really Know Your Customer

A KPP should not be confused with a glorified and glossy quotation or proposal binder with the provocative cash price breakdown hidden in the middle two pages but still 'as bald as a coot' when you get there.

A KPP is not for display with the Customer, it's a culmination of research, in addition to the three-legged stool, six Cs and Rubicon Forcefield Analysis etc, made up from four key sources:

- Sales - previous experience.
- Service, parts and warranty experience plus telematics data (if available).
- Leasing experience and data including credit reference agency data. Statutory accounts analysis, Directors' Strategic Reports, Net Zero performance data, bankers and debt position.
- Other information, mostly from online sources including Customer website, news releases, key personnel positions, and in many cases, almost endless inputs.

It has to be recognised that unlocking the route to promoting advanced services can involve interaction with many traditional internal layers and stakeholders within a Customer's organisation. It is becoming increasingly important to seek out the firm's ESG/sustainability specialists because of growing Net Zero compliance and ambitions.

Once the KPP dossier is assembled an action plan can be put together to ensure that the forthcoming sales approach is briefed to come as close as possible to the knowledge of the Customer representative – but not to be showy. Questions based on the information can be fed out purposely and appropriately to seek confirmation of small pieces – to keep the Customer saying "yes" and sparking curiosity. This broadens the conversation to create the perception that we have sufficient knowledge and expertise to help the Customer/representative recognise that we are the best source of decision help that they could need.

Become the unassailable trading partner for the Customer

The full range of KPP information is not for disclosure, it is there to aid the salesperson or team to better understand wider background to the Customer's situation prior to direct questioning and intensive listening.

Linking this to BE are four issues that make our KPP preparation really powerful because it is being used to:

- Put the Customer at the centre using BE principles and arouse curiosity.
- Understand Customer BE traits in their regular choice of products and services, giving us the ability to identify gaps or previous choices which may not have been made in their operational or financial best interests.
- Help Customers make better decisions which optimise operations and financial handling within their business.
- Enable us to properly understand Customer needs and put forward, in good faith, solutions that better match the desired outcomes.

Proper preparation prevents particularly poor performance! The undisclosed KPP is aiding us, preparing us, to become the unassailable trading partner for the Customer in their potentially serious and imminent capital investment.

Summary & Resources

In this chapter, we've explored how Consultative Finance Language can be made up of a really easy and relaxed sales vocabulary that helps create more perspectives about value. It works best when salespeople become fluent and are able to couple phrases with a good working knowledge of how the numbers work out for different products.

We've linked this to Behavioural Economics and begun to create a Killer Proposition Pack that ensures that a salesperson or team are fully prepared before entering an important sales negotiation.

We've created space to bring the value over time perspective into our Customer conversations.

I am extremely grateful to Mike Ramsay for his help and guidance over many years. Materials supplied by him during the writing of this book and permission to include phrases and techniques to encapsulate 'Consultative Finance Language' were very much appreciated.

https://www.linkedin.com/in/mike-ramsay-457b126/

CHAPTER 13

Rubicon Performance Management

W orking within a sales-aid leasing company taught me that, of course, professional accountancy has a big influence over the whole enterprise. The natural motivation is to run the business 'by the numbers' but there is a paradox here. The 'sales-aid' bit in the company mission means that the majority of the people employed by the business are orientated to help Customers to buy capital equipment. They are salespeople and a strict Financial 1 culture does not offer a good fit to deliver motivation and inspiration.

The Finance 1 Team quite understandably receive job satisfaction from looking at numerical evidence of company performance in all sorts of ways whereas the salespeople tend to be more focused on hitting one or a small number of financial targets (to get paid) but gain most enjoyment of the role through conducting human relations to clinch deals.

One of my old bosses used to say that "selling was the most exciting thing you could do while keeping your clothes on"! He did not have a Finance 1 background. Whereas that attitude would probably be a most daunting thing for many numerically-minded people.

Leasing companies need incredibly intricate financial management. By their very nature, there are no tangible raw materials or finished goods to see, simply invisible money coming in and invisible money going out.

There is a problem with being too focused on analysing the numbers because they mostly relate to things that happened in the past contrasted to a budgeted future best guess. They are reinforced by 'lag indicators' harking back to our earlier story about cheetahs.

"How do we create a good behavioural scorecard?"

Nevertheless, Finance 1 colleagues will tend to place great value on these numbers. The challenge is having the right balance between quantitative and qualitative measurements. Ideally, a sales organisation has to grapple with subjective behavioural inputs and outcomes. Finding a way of expressing them numerically could then supplement the truly financial ones and have them receive the equiv- alent reverence and at the same time give some good 'lead' indicators. We end up with the question "how do we create a meaningful subjective behavioural scorecard?".

Performance Improvement Circle Scorecard (PICS)

I spent a lot of time as a Sales Director working on this issue and came up with a scholarly paper entitled *Leading Performance Improvement in a People Based Business*. The paper majored on a performance improvement scorecard called 'PICS'. It helped me win the UK's Chartered Management Institute's 'Sir Henry Fildes' annual trophy in 2007.

There are four fundamental concepts within PICS:
- A maximum set of eight non-numerical objectives recorded in summary.
- Subjective evidence of achievements against those objectives is recorded.
- An evidence-based performance score -5 to +5.
- A comparison between the previous and current scores aiming to show continuous improvement.

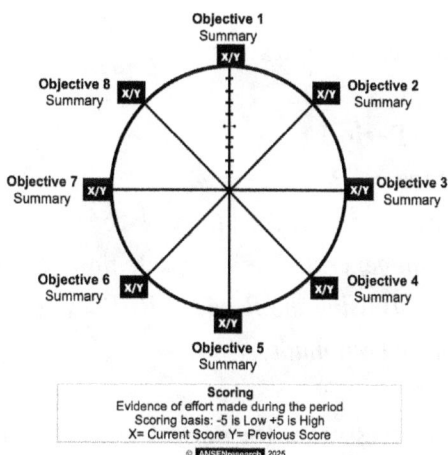

Objective 1
Summary
X/Y

Objective 8
Summary **X/Y**

Objective 2 **X/Y**
Summary

Objective 7 **X/Y**
Summary

Objective 3 **X/Y**
Summary

Objective 6 **X/Y**
Summary

Objective 4 **X/Y**
Summary

X/Y
Objective 5
Summary

Scoring
Evidence of effort made during the period
Scoring basis: -5 is Low +5 is High
X= Current Score Y= Previous Score
© ANSENresearch 2025

Figure 19: PICS Non-Financial Scorecard

A supporting suite of traditional numerical performance data against a limited set of financial targets is also compiled such as turnover, units sold, margins, targets etc. The PICS graphic (see Figure 19) deliberately avoids using a spreadsheet or lists of issues. The idea is to bring a strong visual element to the assessment being made.

A typical objective and summary might be:

Objective 1 - Sales Canvassing
- How consistently has canvassing been practised?
- Have prospects been carefully selected via the Rubicon RFP table?
- Have appropriate records been kept and diary notes been made for future action?
- Has the task been embraced with enthusiasm?
- Have adequate appointments and proposals been generated?

A typical Assessment might be:

Assessment - Period 1
Current Score = +2
The appraisee has approached the task consistently with some enthusiasm and generated an adequate flow of appointments and/or proposals using the Rubicon RFP Table. Appropriate diary notes have been made.

A typical assessment for period two might be:

Assessment - Period 2
Current Score +3, Previous Score +2
The appraisee has benefited from sales canvassing during the previous period and recognised the results of enthusiastic engagement. The commitment to the task has been more thorough with improvements seen in appointments and proposals with some closed deals as a result. Diary notes have been routinely recorded in the Rubicon RFP Table and followed up.

We can then map the current and previous scores on the PICS chart together with up to seven other objectives and performance scores, creating a 'Spider Chart' that gives a broader and immediate perception of how the individual is performing against set objectives.

In the PICS Spider Chart (see Figure 20) we can see that an example summary of Objective 1 –'Canvassing' has been described and a performance score plotted as 3/2 meaning that improvement has been subjectively reviewed and assessed since the previous period.

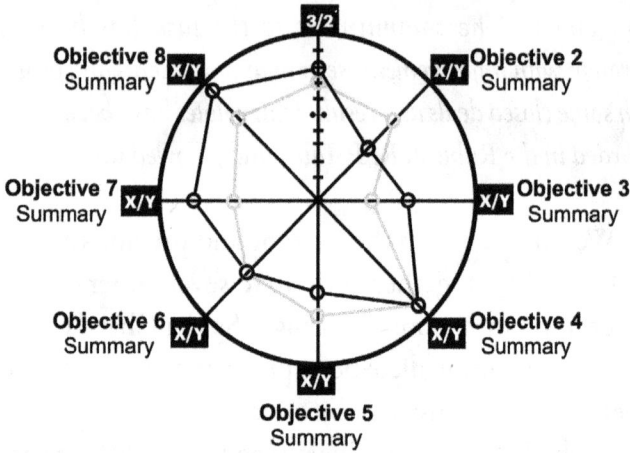

Canvassing
How consistently has canvassing been practiced ?
Have prospects been carefully selected via the Rubicon RFP Table?
Have appropriate records been kept/diary notes been made for future action?
Has the task been embraced with enthusiasm?
Have adequate appointments and proposals been generated?

Scoring
Evidence of effort made during the period
Scoring basis: -5 is Low +5 is High
X= Current Score Y= Previous Score

© ANSENresearch 2025

Figure 20: PICS Example Spider Chart

Other example scores have been plotted to give an idea of how the chart would look with some performances improving but some regressing and in need of attention, whether that be an improved skill or will.

The intention is to focus on attitude and aptitude to determine where extra training or encouragement may be required if scores fall back and especially if negative territory is recorded. A fresh score card is started at the beginning of each year. In the graphic, the latest performance was plotted as darker line, but in reality this would be a succession of colours.

Choosing the Right Performance Objectives

Four additional examples are shown below:

1. Team-working & Inter-Personal Skills

The reason why subjective assessments are important is demonstrated with an objective such as 'Teamworking'. A successful individual may often be judged by 'making the numbers', but their behavioural impact throughout the organisation may be poor and impacting on overall harmony and collaboration, and hamper discretionary effort from co-workers. Equally, the numbers could show good attainment against financial targets, but Customer interaction skills may actually be poor, resulting in sub-optimal flows of potential extra business.

2. Reaction to Change

Another interesting objective could be the depth of 'buy-in' to a special project or business transformation programme. Attitudes and acceptance such as making the move from needing to do what we like to liking what we need to do cannot usually be easily measured in numerical terms.

3. Learning New Skills - Using Sales-Aid Finance

As we saw in earlier chapters, running with a sales-aid finance solution pays dividends but how do members of the Sales Team acquire the skills to deploy this new company asset? The depth of enthusiasm needs to be shown to develop new skills such as sound understanding of leasing key facts and using point of sale Apps to calculate figures smoothly and handling contracts. Not everyone will be able to do this, causing appropriate intervention by HR Partners.

4. Learning New Skills - Transitioning to Selling Advanced Services

If the sales process within a business has relied on a model of capital sales plus parts and some occasional service contracts there will be a considerable amount of learning to be done to reshape the sales process to understand and embrace Advanced Services. This objective will involve abandoning 'cash price' and focus on the value of Customer outcomes. A new vocabulary and language (CFL) will also be required to properly describe what the revised offer is and where value is to be had to Customers who are equally wedded to cash price perceptions (even if they NEVER pay using 'cash'). Not everyone will be able to do this – again, there will be cause for understanding and actions from HR Partners on this vital pivot point.

Achieving a Healthy 'Psychological Contract'

The Psychological Contract[1] is the unwritten, informal agreement that outlines each party's perceived obligations, expectations and beliefs about their working relationship. It's based on assumptions and understandings, rather than formal, legally binding terms. This is where financial performance metrics fall down, and subjective performance measurements become important.

PICS is attempting to discover any disconnects between the appraisee's psychological contract and the mission that is in scope and to help bring about a helpful congruence[2] between self-perception and reality. Discussions become easier as PICS requires supportive evidence to demonstrate buy-in or otherwise to the mission.

Over the years, I've found it quite rare to spot the perfect candidate who possesses the innate abilities to combine equipment types, performance and specifications together with human relations, funding and sales-aid finance skills. Even good players will often know far more detail about their hobbies than some important elements of their jobs. Consequently, there is a need to relentlessly balance internal drivers with coaching and incentives to successfully build and combine sound technical knowledge with human relations skills in a sales role. As businesses orientate to providing advanced services, there is a need to motivate players to enjoy the challenge of looking at longer term success. This could cause a rethink about the levels of basic pay and bonuses to achieve the right balance.

PICS Scorecard – Driving Change

Using PICS means that we've arrived at an ability to measure some more meaningful attributes.

We can move away from simply valuing what we measure to measuring what we value

It is often difficult to handle or quantify subjective performance issues, but PICS gives the ability to move away from simply *valuing what we measure to measuring what we value*. It allows us to move away from placing almost entire reliance on lag financial data to something more useful involving the following:

- PICS can be a low-cost paper-based scorecard that ties into Key Result Areas contained in standard Job Descriptions.
- The non-financial evidence requires hard facts and facilitates opportunities for recognising hard work and job satisfaction not necessarily evident from statistics.
- A lack of supporting evidence indicates poor performance responses in itself.
- The evidence and scores can track return on investment from training and coaching and demonstrates growth (or otherwise) in employee skills and competences.
- The numerical scores convert subjective and qualitative information into quantitative data, useful in an analytical environment where gathering such information is usually regarded as difficult.
- The information provides lead indicators by way of demonstrating the progress of change which should yield the desired results in the near future.
- Performance progress and regression are seen at first hand and zero scores indicate performance stasis which should not be tolerated as the norm.
- Any of the eight behavioural change areas can be

reconfigured to suit prevailing circumstances to provide appropriate focus.

JENZZO Capability & Competencies

Let's head back to Mike and the Plan B Team. They have been working on assessing the four JENZZO competency categories and had created a matrix (see Figure 21).

Core - Classed as inherent within the business and should be maintained and developed.

Maturing - Signalling that these competencies have a limited future lifespan and may not deliver high value within the business in the future. People and systems continuing to cling to these areas will not be well placed in the future set up.

Emerging - These are competencies that will be pivotal to propel the organisation in the future.

Transitional - Competencies that are required to build the bridge between the present and the new way of doing things.

The Plan B Team were keen to bring in the use of the Rubicon PICS and a session was held with the head of HR who was impressed with the new tool and understood the significance of adopting it for the purposes of aiding the change regime that had been laid down by Nicky at a couple of recent JENZZO Exco Meetings. It was well known that people generally do what they are supervised to achieve.

As a result, an HR task force was initiated to draw up plans to identify appropriate external expertise to aid the company, particularly with the transitional competences and also the setting up of some of the emerging competencies. It was noted that future recruitment would need to embed the emerging competencies.

Core	Maturing	Emerging	Transitional
Quality Engineering	Cash Price Trading	Outcome Based Solutions	Training & Coaching
Product R&D	Transactional Focus	Relationship & Pipeline Focus	New Financial Performance Analysis
Equipment Features & Benefits Data	Cost Plus Design & Planned Obsolescence	Sales-Aid Finance Partnership and Methods	Re-work Warranty & Service Costs
HR – Team Development Management including AI	JENZZO 'versus' software	Contractual Comprehension & Pricing Specialism	New Risk Analysis
Internal & External Comms	Service Data Spreadsheets	Mobile IT, AI, Internal and Customer Apps	Reduce Multiple Profit Centres
Performance Management	Product Over-Complexity	Asset Management & Residual Values	Stakeholder Management & Comms
Parts & Service Supply		Assessing Needs & Behavioural Economics	New Invoicing Reconciliation
Marketing & Brand Management		Product Design for Outcomes	Reconfigure Service & Parts Ops
Cost Control		Telematics – Monetising Know-How	Legal Contract Drafting
Effective Procurement		CRM including Rubicon RFP	
		Service Response Efficiency	

Figure 21: JENZZO Capability & Competencies Assessment

Internal communications regarding the shift to advanced services had already begun and workshops had been formed in various departments to act as forums for ideas generation and Q&A sessions to bring out any fears or concerns that might exist. Several other projects had been deferred to allow for Plan B progress to be prioritised.

Sales Incentives – A New Regime

The Sales Team financial incentives had always been based on a formula related to the margin achieved above ex-works prices achieved. The move to advanced services and outcome-based contracts would see an end to that tried and tested (and stale) incentives system – there would have to be an honourable funeral for the old regime. In future, there would be two streams.

Incentive Stream 1 – Sales Commissions

The first would relate to a notional 'Inception Profitability' (IP) figure aligned to each advanced services contract 'sale' and the second being a notional 'thank you' from JENZZO ASC for introducing and completing the funding underlying the contract set.

The first 18 months from the switch would involve some smoothing of sales commissions that would offer reassurance that income levels, and therefore lifestyles, were not going to be subjected to immediate turbulence. This was not going to be a cost saving exercise at the expense of the salesforce. A rebalancing of basic pay versus bonuses would also have to be undertaken to emphasise the move to longer term behaviours.

After that, the new scheme would be based on the overall potential income from medium- to long-term contracts. Notional IP income figures would be used so that individual deal intricacies would not overwhelm the intentions of the scheme.

Each salesperson would receive an annual IP target attached to a quarterly 'banking' system. The annual target would be broken down to quarterly segments with seasonal adjustments. Pre-defined incentives would begin at 80% of target and awards would accelerate up to 100% and beyond to a maximum of 115%. The financial awards would be credited to an individual account and be guaranteed to be payable three months after the end of the financial year. This would give time for another bankable quarter to be accomplished and so lessen the chance of individuals walking away with their year-end bonus because they would forfeit the bonus 'banked' in the new quarter. If there was an underscore in any of the four quarters, an over-rider would be payable if 100% of the annual target was achieved at the year-end, thus wiping out a low quarterly score.

Incentive Stream 2 – Funder Commissions

Using the services of an external incentives operator, JENZZO ASC would create an individual Visa or Mastercard debit card account for each salesperson and awards made for successful completion of deals involving JENZZO ASC would be credited straightaway to each card account. The awards ranged from €50 to €150 per whole goods transacted up to an annual limit of 30 awards per Customer account. Each award would be paid net of local taxes. The debit cards were usable worldwide, but cash could not be withdrawn as part of the scheme rules. The scheme provider would run online accounts for any active participant and provide appropriate local tax certification to the holder and the JENZZO CFO.

The debit card could also act as a platform, eg for cementing the switch to advanced services with short term incentives or 'Snap Competitions' run by any part of JENZZO to motivate certain behaviours.

Summary & Resources

In this chapter we've seen a way to move from almost complete reliance on financial data as a performance indicator to a new scorecard placing emphasis on subjective performance assessments carrying a numerical score.

In the context of transforming a business into providing advanced services, the PICS system is aimed at delivering a platform for coaching performance improvement and injecting inspiration and high esteem to achieve the pivotal move to understand, engage and sell advanced services contracts.

[1] *Psychological Contract*
https://www.personio.com/hr-lexicon/psychological-contract-explained/

[2] *Congruence*
https://en.wikipedia.org/wiki/Carl_Rogers

CHAPTER 14

Selling in a Service-Based Way

This is where we bring all of the elements together to enable an advanced services offer to come to life and a Customer proposition to be made and upheld.

In the past, I've found it quite an interesting task to form a 'Trio of Actors' (see Figure 22) within a business and put them in a room together.

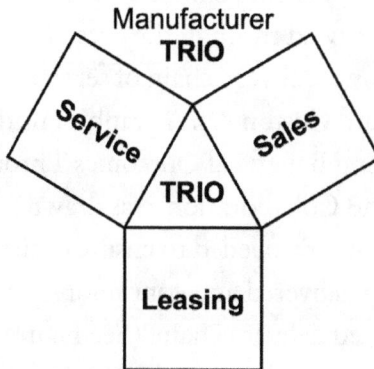

Figure 22: Manufacturer TRIO Actors

The actors being members of the Customer-facing teams from Sales, Service and Finance 2. It can be quite a shock to discover that bringing together cross-functional people like this can be a rare event and much can be learned from the revealing discussions that take place.

The deliberate blurring of sales and post-sales responsibilities takes considerable effort and trust so that satisfying the Customer and delivering on promises becomes the single objective, moving away from one-off transactions to relationship-based trading which helps to build a holistic view of delivering outcomes.

This, in a nutshell, can be the route to creating and sustaining beneficial outcomes through Customer-facing practitioners and then receiving feedback to create and improve services and products that continuously deliver even more valuable benefits.

Mike and the JENZZO Plan B Team began this 'TRIO' practice midway through their project work, and much benefit was derived such as:

- Mapping the existing and new sales processes, especially viewed through the eyes of a Customer and their own delivery chain of services provided to their onward Customers. A graphic entitled 'Creating & Sustaining Beneficial Outcomes Through End-to-End Collaboration' was drawn up to show the information flow needed to ensure desired outcomes were being delivered and continuously perfected from this extended delivery chain. (See Figure 23)
- The Plan B Team had been advised by Nicky that the JENZZO Board and C Bank had agreed to form

a JV and much work had been undertaken to bring this to life including appointing key staff. C Bank and C Leasing had been instrumental in achieving this work. A new recruit called Sasha would lead the new JV and become intricately involved in the work of the TRIO. Sylvia was very pleased to be recruited into the JV too.

- A new post of 'Pricing Specialism' had been created which also included oversight and deployment of BE principles and contract innovation simplified through use of bespoke point of sale Apps including 'Value Quantification Guides' to aid explanations of outcome benefits.

Creating & Sustaining Beneficial Outcomes Through End-to-End Collaboration

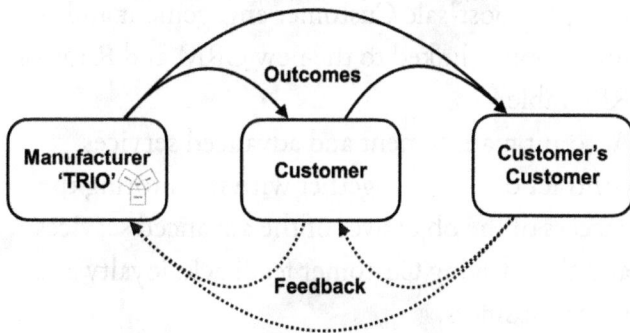

© ANSENresearch 2025

Figure 23: Creating & Sustaining Beneficial Outcomes Through End-to-End Collaboration

- A TRIO gap analysis of Customer-facing capabilities recognising that there will be a mix of innate skill orientations. This work migrated to Key Performance Indicators (KPI) within Job Descriptions and was integrated into the PICS Scorecards to ensure alignment of Plan B/TRIO objectives and a range of relevant financial incentives.
- Lifting sales skills including financial and product features and benefits and roll-out of CFL coaching leading to a comprehensive 'Know How' guides that could be integrated into point of sale Apps with pop-up AI assistance to aid learning.
- Lifting inter-personal and contractual awareness skills – no more gossip misdemeanours with Customers like "Oh, we have a lot of trouble with this model"!
- Mapping post-sale Customer engagement and touch points linked to the new CRM and Rubicon RFP table.
- Account management and advanced services contract oversight together with monitoring the success of the objectives of the advanced services and thus driving Customer feedback, loyalty and repeat business.
- Telematics dashboards including various states of priority actions and Customer information services including feedback to engineering designers.
- A new post of Advanced Services 'Tsar' was created and this function would include quality audits, regular physical equipment inspections, fitness for

purpose assessments and any important health and safety concerns, plus reporting back any equipment abuse and product design or engineering issues for follow up actions.

Dual Business Model

Using the Customer Segregation Matrix, the team reluctantly recommended a dual business model to allow for limited continuation of new business on traditional terms. In-depth training of handling the twin types of business flows would avoid a duplication of TRIO resources and extra cost.

The dual model was a pragmatic recognition of the characteristics of the 'Genghis Khan' pricing terrorist who would still acquire volume equipment but would only purchase at the lowest possible cash price, use spurious aftermarket spare parts and would not opt for telematics or outcomes-based treatment. Even if they did, nothing would ever be right and lead to high cost and unproductive case management.

Sylvia came out with a sharp assessment – "This segment is born not to trust, they expect to be treated as they would treat the world. It is best not to trust them either! When dealing with such a Customer we've found it better to handle them from a direct sales desk rather than face-to-face, not just because of the cost, but perversely, we've seen that we can obtain better margins by not being bullied face-to-face!" This caused quite a smile around the TRIO table, especially with Sasha!

The 'Collaborators' segment were the best target for advanced services contracts followed by the 'Brand Addicts'. Customer focus groups had been set up to test ideas and shape contract offerings. There were possibilities of obtaining better margins by identifying where advanced services could also deliver in-use value to their onward Customers' operations.

The occasional or 'cash' Customers would be provided with options to take up advanced services via physical or online marketing materials held by the sales staff, dependent on the degree of sophistication of the Customer.

For the time being, the dual model approach would also mitigate some of the impact caused by reorientation of immediate income from pure sales transactions to longer term annuitised earnings from services which suited the internal Finance 1 department. The pragmatic approach would therefore smooth the journey to *Crossing the Rubicon*.

Advance Services – Contractual Offer

The obvious key questions were 'what is going to be the advanced services offer?' and 'what is the Customer going to get?'.

It made sense to move the JENZZO Internal Counsel closer to the frontline to help with the design of the contracts and to continue to act in close quarters with the TRIO teams to ensure a high degree of agility to handle legal and regulatory compliance in cases where customising work would be needed.

In JENZZO's case the initial services were based on a new comprehensive site and application survey which, in part, drew on the Killer Proposition Pack augmented by further findings during the in-depth negotiations. The basic contract provided:

- Guaranteed up-times with rebates for non-performance of response times with 24/7 cover.
- Various novel services derived from the telematics data (see below).
- Guaranteed energy savings compared to existing kit to aid Customer Net Zero compliance meeting IFRS standards.
- An optional two-month payment pause each year to cope with seasonality, intermittent tariff actions or supply chain interruptions at ports etc.
- Access to a new online portal for self-ordering consumables such as oil, grease and other wearing parts together with feedback from telematics on potential 'style of usage' savings to reduce fuel consumption and excessive wear and tear.
- Exploration of off-balance sheet financial treatment for the Customer meeting IFRS standards.

Telematics Command Centre

A Telematics Command Centre was set up to handle all aspects of running Telematics subscriptions for the length of the contract that provided Apps and online account access in addition to the usual machine operational status data including:

- Equipment location – this had the added benefit of lowering the risk of theft faced by JENZZO ASC and insurance companies who were often able to reduce their premiums as a result.
- Geo-fencing capability. One Customer previously had a machine go missing, presumed to be on the high seas, inside a ship's hold!
- Out of contracted hours usage alerts.
- RAG status providing equipment health reports.
- Operator abuse of equipment and excessive speeds or load alerts.
- Hours of use, cycles or volume meter readings – this aided oversight of depreciation curves and gave options to charge out on a per-hour/cycle basis in the near future.
- AI-driven 360° proximity cameras distinguishing human and non-human near misses and impacts (recorded and alerts issued).
- Head-Up Displays for equipment operators aligned to the preordained working tasks and performance envelopes.
- Movement records and travel maps providing data for efficiency savings eg on an airport apron, dockside or railhead.
- Facial recognition of operators to aid security where necessary.
- An equipment operator smartphone App to record completion of daily checks such as fuel, oil, temperature, vibration, fastenings, hydraulic pressures, tyre pressures, water coolant, greasing,

lighting, hygiene and any other required hardware inspections. This was all passed back to the Customer's dashboard.

- Visual Reality (VR) enabled engineers based within the Telematics Command Centre were available to aid simple local equipment optimisation adjustments or fixes without the need for delays in physical service call-outs.
- API-enabled Data flows to the Customer to provide real-time records of hours used, volumes produced or loads shifted to tie in with their onward billing.
- There was a recognition that Telematics, APIs and AI would need balancing by human intervention to maintain the vital depth of relationships with Customers – it would not be a 'fire and forget' operation.

An interesting commitment was made in some contracts to provide existing Customers with an option to swap out diesel-driven equipment when JENZZO's R&D ('Black Ops') Team were confident about commencing production of battery electric and hydrogen powered equipment. Work had also begun on shaping the facilitation of 'green' hydrogen gas produced via renewable energy on supply contracts with the growing number of infrastructure and supply specialists.

Within the remit of the Internal Counsel, JENZZO ASC became the central hub to control or supervise all elements of contractual, risk sharing, legal, regulatory and communication with the Customer and it supplied electronic all-inclusive monthly invoices for all matters relating to the use of the equipment. This dampened communication overload by various separate departments. Reconciliation of payment components of finance and service, maintenance, repair (chargeable and non-chargeable), consumables, supplementary telematics charges and any third-party costs were undertaken.

To aid repeatability and scalability, the advanced services contract structure was designed as modular with a suite of standard components drawn up to suit various Customer and usage circumstances. Any deviations were handled by the new role of the Pricing Specialist who had direct contact with JENZZO's internal Legal Counsel and their exterior lawyers across the regions served. A sub-committee of the JENZZO Main Board would be available at short notice if risk assessments showed that proposed bespoke clauses or recourse undertakings went beyond pre-agreed remits. The Pricing Specialist was encouraged to be creative about charging mechanisms and quickly set to work with Sam to see how far the innovation envelope could be expanded and new 'as-a-Service' Systems were soon on the drawing board. Sasha was also keen to explore Monthly Revenue Recognition models with C Bank's New Products Department who had a couple of pilot schemes taking place with another manufacturer which enabled debt to be removed from their balance sheet and that of the Customer.

Lift as-a-Service Pilot Scheme

A new charge-out system was being piloted with a collaborative Customer based in the multi-modal logistics sector. This involved loading and unloading cargo containers between trucks and trains at a railhead using a JENZZO 'Rubber-Tyred Gantry' (RTG) crane [1].

The proposed contract pricing structure was based on an expected number of lift movements (Cycles) over the crane usage span of up to ten years with the average expected to be 100 Cycles per day. Based on historical data, this worked out at around 2,600 Cycles per month.

The JENZZO ASC proposal had three monthly Cycle Allocation options for consideration. It was known informally as the *'Snake in the Tunnel'* charging system. The Customer could select the Allocation quote they felt best suited their averages and, importantly, their peaks and troughs.

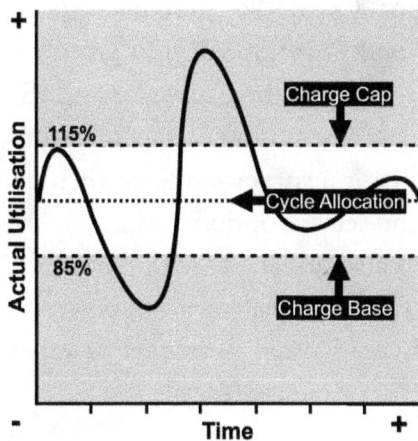

Figure 24: Pilot Charge-Out System

The selected Allocation would be entered into the contract (see Figure 24):

Quote 1 – Cycle Allocation: 2,200 @ €X per cycle
Quote 2 – Cycle Allocation: 2,600 @ €Y per cycle
Quote 3 – Cycle Allocation: 3,000 @ €Z per cycle

A monthly 'Charge Base' was set at 85% of the chosen Cycle Allocation level.

A monthly 'Charge Cap' was set at 115% of the chosen Cycle Allocation level, above which no additional charges would be levied.

Each monthly invoice covered all necessary elements including funding, repair & maintenance service plans, consumables, telematics services, tyre inspections/replacements and lifting inspections. The monthly charge would be adjusted in line with the actual use in accordance with the above Base and Cap parameters.

An annual reconciliation would take place to ensure that the original Cycle Allocation met expected levels.

The **Sprinter** Point-of-Sale CPQ App was updated to provide the ability for the Customer and JENZZO Sales Specialist to agree equipment specifications based on a site and application survey data and then plan the Cycle Allocations and service options.

Work was also underway within the JENZZO 'Black Ops' Team to look at replacing diesel power with hydrogen or battery hybrid power systems to meet increasing demands for Net Zero credentials

Sales-Aid Finance JV Framework Considerations

A framework contract had been drawn up between C Bank, JENZZO ASC and JENZZO Group, linked to the main JV Agreement, detailing the ownership of the various important risks. Sasha was keen to make sure that C Bank and its subsidiary, JENZZO ASC, would not be taking on a disproportionate amount of risks in addition to traditional Customer credit and equipment residual value risks. These included various tasks associated with integrating the telematics and service performance undertakings, communications and billing which required formal written undertakings from JENZZO Group. There would also need to be acceptable compensation in consideration of the duties now being expected from JENZZO ASC. The 'Snake in the Tunnel' charge-out system being a good example.

JENZZO Progress & Outcomes

The Sales Team at JENZZO Group had arrived at the crucial moment. The Plan B Team were delivering their transformative impact on the business. Together with Lindsay, Amy and the marketing team, the Customer segments have been identified, focus group feedback had been received, target market sectors had been researched and the first most appropriate JENZZO product range and models have been selected for promotion on the new advanced services contract terms.

The Sales Team had received in-depth training and begun their own canvassing work using the new RFP tables with many KPPs already compiled and 'live' prospects identified. Speculative proposals were beginning to appear on the new CRM pipeline system. POS CPQ Apps supplied by Sylvia and the new JENZZO ASC Team had been loaded with JENZZO product and funding templates and data.

The Sales Team now knew that they were to lead Customer conversations using a brand new and persuasive vocabulary with good alignment to BE to create opportunities. They could be confident to have fairly fuzzy initial talks attempting to draw out issues and offer possible solutions that the Customer had perhaps never considered before. This would go beyond the mere performance of equipment and would stray into the evolution of such things as embracing Net Zero opportunities and combating a growing threat of low-cost imports.

Their confidence was boosted further by some amazing insights provided by the new telematics system. Conversations would be about identifying problems, creating a need and then coming up with advanced services solutions. A mental deal funnel would help to cast away unnecessary flotsam that had little relevance to helping the Customer to make a positive decision about buying into advanced services deprioritise other work.

Sales success stories would be shared on an internal blog for use by colleagues and league tables would highlight progress. The Service Team would be co-creating solutions and own the performance-to-contract obligations and constantly pass crucial equipment development ideas back to Todd and the designers and engineers. Sasha and the JENZZO ASC Team would be managing the 'never-ending' transactions and highlighting any new buying signals along the way, and new forms of charging contracts were being piloted. Market surveys and a new NPS system and the PICS scorecard would reveal to Nicky and sales management important and swift course corrections along the way.

During the project build up phase, the JENZZO ExCo had become very aligned to the strategic change and Nicky, Lindsay, Charlie, Robin and Nico were very appreciative of the Plan B Team's work led by Mike.

They Crossed the Rubicon

Summary & Resources

In this chapter we brought together the main Customer facing entities of Sales, Service and Leasing to form a TRIO of understanding.

From now on, the JENZZO TRIO will blur their traditional roles and focus on the outcomes that suit their Customers' ultimate needs. They will *Cross the Rubicon* and stop the concentration on pure features and benefits and performance linked to cash prices of their equipment.

Some of the guaranteed outcomes will no doubt be very novel to Customers because the new servitization model should aid the search for ways to collaborate and produce better outcomes via a new range of Advanced Services.

[1] *Report for BNSF Railyard Operations: Rubber-Tyred Gantry Cranes - Zero and near Zero Emission Freight Facilities in California*
https://ww2.arb.ca.gov/sites/default/files/2022-11/zanzeff-bnsf-rtgreport.pdf

Conclusion

In summing up the research, personal insights and storytelling, contained in this book, I hope that I've added some interesting dimensions to consider when implementing Servitization.

The extremely important topics of R&D, design, procurement, service network capability and other operational matters have received a light touch. There are many research papers and books written by experts that offer guidance and superb models in these areas.

I have tried, in the main, to stick to what I know best – sales-aid finance and integrating service contracts alongside cultural and performance management to cover what I feel may sometimes be neglected topics when manufacturers transition to Servitization.

Today, there is a combination of factors that should be driving manufacturers and their Customers to collaborate far more deeply to achieve better outcomes to boost productivity and returns.

The key pressures that have rippled through these chapters are as follows:

1. The rise of onboard sensors and telematics together with systems enabling insights going far beyond performance and condition will propel manufacturers and Customers to reimagine the value-added services that could provide strategic and tactical advantage in

an increasingly aggressive and contended marketplace.

2. Consequences of a change in the traditional global trading order, caused by new tariff measures introduced by the USA, will see trade in manufactured goods deflecting away from that market. Uncertainty will cause these finished products to divert to other developed economies, causing an increase in tension and threat to domestic manufacturers and their suppliers.

3. Net Zero drivers are not within the total control of governments. Various actors will play an increasing part in shaping, ratcheting and pressuring how manufacturers and their stakeholders and Customers will need to respond.

4. Business transformation will be necessary to move away from the traditional equipment sales and aftercare model to one that embraces what the Customer is trying to achieve, often involving their own onward Customers. The emerging models will require a different approach to many parts of a manufacturer's operations and my core interest has focused mainly on internal cultural change, funding capability, selling skills and performance management to equip firms to win by delivering Advanced Services.

Summary and Resources
It is my belief that Servitization offers the prime route to both DEFEND and GROW in today's market.

Each one of the four drivers mentioned in this Conclusion may seem to have a different timeline but the sooner manufacturers recognise and act to face this uncertain future the quicker they will become more resilient and avoid a potentially catastrophic price discounting war by transitioning to grow by *transforming products into services.*

Advanced Services Group
I strongly recommend that readers reach out to the Advanced Services Group Ltd who are globally acknowledged Servitization experts:

https://www.advancedservicesgroup.co.uk/

See also the following books:
Made to Serve
Baines & Howard. Wiley.
ISBN: 9781118585313

Serivization Strategy
Baines, Bigdelli, Kapoor. Palgrave Macmillan.
ISBN 9783031454288

CHAPTER 15

Epilogue

The picture of transforming a business trading model into one of Servitization has, by necessity, been simplified in a number of ways.

Firstly, I have not included in the model, to any extent, a business that is trading through an independent and fairly powerful network of dealers, neither have we examined the complexity of intermediaries such as rental companies operating in the short- or medium-term hire sector that can stand between the manufacturer, its dealers and the ultimate user.

Dealer Networks

Manufacturers pay a great deal of attention to forming their dealer networks and attempt to create a stable distribution platform to act as a reliable sales and after-market channel. This may involve serious investment by both parties and tensions regarding volume, margins, business development, market share, brand projection and protection etc. In this scenario the manufacturer relies on the expertise of the dealer to deliver an acceptable level of service, maintenance and breakdown capability to keep their joint Customers' equipment in good order.

Attempting to introduce Servitization within this environment adds considerable complexity, such as competing agendas, differing cultures, shareholder expectations, investment appetites and varied levels of capabilities and skills from management to sales and after-market staff across the network.

In response to this, some manufacturers, especially in the automotive sector, have decided to build their own distribution network and dispense with independent dealers, but this may not always lead to success and requires serious investment and risk-taking, particularly if existing dealers have strong and long-term relationships with their Customers. This traditional separation does, however, provide a degree of legal and contractual 'buffer' between the manufacturer and the Customer.

Running a manufacturing organisation versus running dealerships requires very different capabilities.

Rental Businesses

My background has given me a ring-side seat within the UK's construction machinery rental sector. Rental companies have been consolidating and growing enormously in many markets over the years and moved away from being the SME regional players of the past to becoming nationwide and international operators underpinning major infrastructure developments.

Large construction and housebuilding firms often do not hold their own fleets of construction machinery but rely on large rental firms to support their construction projects which allows the mix of machinery to change as projects develop from ground-breaking to final fitting out.

In many markets, this situation has placed rental firms as the prominent buyers of manufacturers' products and positioned them as already providing forms of advanced services to end users. They would likely regard any manufacturer's move into advanced services as hostile territory and dent their appetite to continue to buy equipment from that supplier and take their considerable trade elsewhere.

Also, it is likely that a rental company will not operate with a programme of using only one manufacturer's equipment within their fleet which, over time, causes a manufacturer's route to market to become dominated by the rental intermediary which can cause extreme pressure on pricing, margins, volumes and market share. The situation can also cause issues with equipment innovation because rental businesses operate in a very aggressive price driven sector and often tend to prefer fairly simple equipment rather than risk taking on innovative and more costly equipment.

Manufacturers trading in rental-dominated sectors have difficult decisions to make in order to defend and grow their businesses, especially if the route to the end user becomes untenable.

Asset Finance

The availability of asset finance around the world differs

considerably. Manufacturers using leasing facilities rarely have a single formula that works across different regions and so the adoption of a mixture of loose partnerships or captive, vendor or joint venture solutions are regularly deployed to suit local conditions. Our fictional 'JENZZO' example ultimately involved an unusual joint venture with an international bank but local regulations and practices would still likely cause fluctuations in how advanced services contracts could be put together and delivered. Separate solutions would have to be arranged in those countries without representation from the chosen JV bank partner. This multiplies the complexity of operations but there is still a need for external financial muscle to underpin the capital funding needs of providing advanced services.

The Revolving Door

Nowadays, more than ever in the real world, businesses have to contend with the 'revolving door' of senior and talented people moving between job to job. What goes for strategy today can become toast tomorrow either within manufacturers or their Customers.

In which case '*Crossing the Rubicon*' may appear less permanent, although moving to a Servitization business model, involving long-term contracts and obligations, means there is a long tail of issues that cannot be 'turned off' and a new direction be adopted at the drop of a hat, usually by both contracting parties.

About the Author

Paul Jennings is keen to share his experience of a life-long career in business, starting with humble beginnings, no university education and with little self-confidence or expertise.

His progress benefited from receiving mentoring, generously given (often unknowingly) by others, plus observing good and not so good management styles practised by hundreds of people striving to figure out the art of running a business.

By building on his personal mantra of *enthusiasm, hard-work and honesty,* he created an authentic style fostering trust and garnering followers that saw him ultimately receive national awards and fellowships, a Visiting Professorship and an invitation to 10 Downing Street – all way beyond the comprehension of those early years after leaving school at the age of fifteen.

Here lies the germ of eagerness to share the learnings, systems and models that can aid the pursuit of constant business transformation which is increasingly important in the writhing and restless economies of today.

This experience prompted the foundation of the partnership consultancy, **ANSENresearch.**

www. ansenresearch.co.uk

Index

www.ingramcontent.com/pod-product-compliance
Lightning Source LLC
Chambersburg PA
CBHW061147220326
41599CB00025B/4390

* 9 7 8 1 9 1 8 0 7 7 4 2 1 *